INTENTION

"Intention is a superpower which when used correctly aligns us to our purpose and helps fulfil our heart's work. Andrew Wallas elegantly and generously shows us how. His approach is simple, yet it is not easy – but boy is it worth it."

Emma Cannon, fertility and women's health expert, acupuncturist and author of *Fertile*

"It is a joy to find a life-changing book that is so clearly and beautifully written. Andrew Wallas distils decades of clinical practice with wisdom and a deceptively light touch. The overall message is strong. We are each responsible for our own path to happiness, and *Intention* is the inspiring guidebook that can help us to find it."

Georgia Coleridge, author of *The Chakra Project*

Andrew Wallas

INTENTION

*How to Tap into the Most
Underrated Power in the Universe
to Create the Life You Want*

aster

An Hachette UK Company
www.hachette.co.uk

First published in Great Britain in 2019 by Aster, an imprint of
Octopus Publishing Group Ltd
Carmelite House
50 Victoria Embankment
London EC4Y 0DZ
www.octopusbooks.co.uk

Distributed in the US byHachette Book Group,1290 Avenue of the
Americas, 4th and 5th Floors, New York, NY 10104
Distributed in Canada by Canadian Manda Group, 664 Annette St.
Toronto, Ontario, Canada M6S 2C8

ISBN 978-1-78325-316-6

A CIP catalogue record for this book is available from the British Library.
Printed and bound in the UK
10 9 8 7 6 5 4 3 2 1

Consultant Publisher: Kate Adams
Senior Editor: Sophie Elletson
Art Director: Juliette Norsworthy
Production Manager: Lisa Pinnell
Illustrations: Ella Mclean

For Anna

CONTENTS

ONE

SEED

Intention is probably the most underrated and misunderstood phenomenon in terms of fulfilling potential and creating the life you want. Nothing in the universe exists without intention. The house you live in, the car you drive, the clothes you wear, the relationships in your life and your favourite music cannot exist without intention. Even you do not exist without intention. Intention is the creative power that fulfils our dreams. An intention is an inner impulse that is focused in a particular direction and contains within it the seed of that which you seek to create. Just like real seeds, intentions can grow or perish according to the fertility of the soil and the attention they receive. Intention orchestrates infinite possibility and is the DNA of all reality.

Intention is not desire. Desires arise throughout the day – the desire for a drink or for food, the desire to sit and relax or the desire to go for a walk. Desires are temporary and fall away again, whether they are satisfied or not – they are transient. Intention is permanent and arises from deep within us. It maintains a focus that is not easily diverted.

Most of us are familiar with goal setting in either a work or personal scenario, or both. Intention is very different from setting goals. Goals can be useful. They have their place, especially if you focus on the outcome, knowing with absolute clarity the result that you want to achieve. This can be very motivational for some people, and can help to set the direction of travel. Goals are rational, logical, linear, task-orientated and left-brain focused. They can be effective and bring about modest success, but in my experience, they are limited and frequently don't work.

This is because goals are set using only a part of our conscious mind (the left brain). Hence, in pursuing them we are operating on just 50 per cent of our potential from the conscious part of our mind. In addition, by relying on the conscious mind, we fail to consider any unconscious resistance. When we are working towards a goal, if we encounter any form of resistance, we simply keep on re-affirming the goal, which denies (represses) the resistance and makes it less likely that we will achieve the goal – what you resist persists (see Chapter Four, Weeds).

Discovery of an intention goes much deeper than goal setting, and is more profound. It integrates left and right brain, and is more holistic. An intention is the energetic starting point of any goal in its purest form. It is the seed that creates the magnificent flower. It's a powerfully authentic vow that you make with yourself, which comes from your core. Once we have articulated the intention, we expect and welcome resistance and integrate it when it arises. The resistance or doubt is in this way transformed, making the intention more powerful.

The life that you are living right now is the way that it is because of intention. Whether you recognize it or not, you are creating the life you are living through the power of intention. As individuals we spend our lives rearranging the furniture of the outer world, constantly surprised that the overall outcome never changes that much. We leave one job and get another one. We leave one relationship and start another one with someone who seems completely different. We move houses and maybe we move countries but we always take ourselves with us. Rather than taking responsibility for the life we are creating, we have become conditioned to blaming other people and circumstances in the outer world for the life we are living. If married or in a committed relationship, we regularly blame our spouse or partner; we blame other people's failings; we blame national events; we blame global events; and, of course, we even blame the weather for feeling miserable. The hard reality is that blaming anyone or anything outside ourselves for how we are living our life or how we are feeling within ourselves is a dead end. There are no exceptions to this. The alternative is to take responsibility for our experiences and learn how to create a different reality.

This is incredibly simple. However, it is far from easy because the shift from making someone or something else responsible to taking responsibility and accepting accountability requires us to move through layer upon layer of conditioning. We have created many different cultures, all of which display a disturbing and relentless lack of responsibility and accountability at the current time. Individuals are reluctant to take responsibility for simple errors or for their actions, preferring to pass the buck to someone or something else. Against this background, embracing radical responsibility is challenging but it is a prerequisite for change. It is the price we have to pay for creating a different life.

In every religious and spiritual tradition, the Devil, Satan, Lucifer is personified by the lie. It seems to me that this is highly appropriate. Whatever we may understand by such a darkly seductive figure, it leads us away from the truth and from a deep connection with ourselves. Several years ago, I took some time to sit and reflect upon the question: 'What is the greatest lie of human existence?' As human beings we are constantly lying to ourselves on a daily basis. We have many layers of self-delusion and denial. In my enquiry, I was interested to delve below the surface layers to reach the lie that inflicts the most damage. The answer I reached was that the greatest lie of the

The greatest lie
of the human
species is the
attractive idea
that someone or
something outside
of ourselves can
make us happy.

human species is the attractive idea or thought that someone or something outside of ourselves can make us happy. It cannot be understated how widespread and pernicious this belief is. It operates in our lives every day in a myriad of ways, completely undermining the fabric of the life we want to create.

I recognized this as a compulsive delusion over 20 years ago, but if I am honest enough or attentive enough, I still catch myself on a daily basis wanting to blame my wife for my dissatisfaction. The difference now from several years ago is that I indulge the distortion for less time before I get back on track and remind myself that I am the author of my own destiny. The best analogy for the shift that needs to take place is to imagine that you are sitting in a cinema watching a film of your life unfold. You get to a part that you would rather not witness, possibly a major rejection or betrayal that was incredibly painful. You walk out of the cinema, shake it off and go to another cinema in a neighbouring town, expecting to see a different version of your life unfold. You sit down and discover that it is the same film at exactly the same place in your life. You immediately leap up, walk out of the cinema, travel to a different country, sit in the foreign cinema and once again it is the same film playing. Why is this the case?

It is because we are the projector and the life we are living is the screen upon which we create and live out our drama. Most of us spend the majority of our time seeking to change the outer detail of our lives. We drop some friends, make new friends, change lovers, make radical lifestyle shifts, thinking that this will change our reality and how we feel. It is critical to understand that this is like going to the cinema and watching *Titanic*, getting out of our seat, walking over to the screen and trying to change the characters and what they are doing. The action is absurd and yet this is precisely how we are conducting our lives. Until we understand the veracity of this we will not make the shift required. If, instead of seeking to change the images on the screen, we go behind the projector, remove the film that is playing and insert a new film, we immediately get a different image on the screen. It is precisely the same with our lives. The new film in the projector is the seed of intention.

If you plant a pumpkin seed, you get a pumpkin. If you plant a carrot seed, you get a carrot. If you place *The Matrix* in the projector you get *The Matrix* on the screen. The life we are living right now is the consequence of the seed we have planted for ourselves. Trying to change the consequences is like trying to grow a pumpkin from a carrot seed. We need to take a step back and assume responsibility for the seed that we have planted. The beautiful simplicity of this truth is that any time we want to discover what the seed of our intention is, we only have to look at our reality. Our current reality is constantly providing us with valuable data similar to a biofeedback loop. If we are living a miserable life, or we are unsuccessful in our career, that is the intention that we have set for ourselves. It is difficult for all of us to accept or acknowledge this idea because we can't believe that we would create something unwelcome and unpalatable for ourselves. The result is that we keep creating more misery and more career failure. The ingenious way this works is that by refusing to take responsibility for it, we continue to create the undesired outcome and get to blame someone else for our misfortune.

If you plant a pumpkin seed, you get a pumpkin.

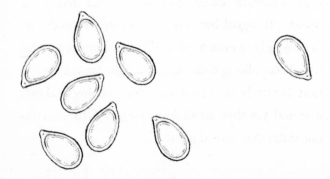

～

In order to understand this fully, we need to differentiate between the conscious mind and the unconscious mind. This is exemplified by the image of an iceberg. The visible part is enormous but compared with the part underneath the water line, which is unseen, it is a fraction of the overall iceberg. Psychologists from radically different traditions and models agree that our conscious mind constitutes around 5–10 per cent of our potential awareness, whereas the unconscious mind, which is outside of our awareness, represents 90–95 per cent of the whole. Understanding this helps us to make sense of a number of practical illustrations. For example, an obese individual might set an intention to lose 20–25kg (45–55 stone) in weight. Consciously, he exerts great energy and dedication towards this goal but several years later remains the same weight or even heavier. We all know people who have been talking about losing weight for years – the next diet or the next exercise regime is going to clinch it – and yet they never lose weight. This scenario illustrates two critical points.

Firstly, it is always remarkable how such people avoid taking responsibility for themselves. Secondly, and more importantly, despite all their conscious effort, something else is undermining their best endeavours. We are all familiar with this dynamic of setting an intention that we never quite achieve despite increasing levels of effort.

Not taking responsibility is reflected by giving up too easily, thoughts and feelings of: 'It's all too hard for me, it's all too difficult.' There is a lack of discipline and a lack of motivation. Many people give in at the first challenge.

In contrast, taking responsibility is understanding that challenges will arise which might be difficult. But there is a willingness to move through the challenge in the awareness that fulfilling the intention is more important. It means focusing on the longer-term benefit rather than instant gratification.

In over 30 years of clinical practice, I have seen numerous men and women who are single vociferously maintain that they want a relationship. Many of them have joined dating agencies, go to every party they are invited to and are constantly looking for the ideal partner, but remain single. The starting point for any enquiry or attempt to support individuals with this issue is to face the self-evident truth that 51 per cent or more of their intention does not want a relationship and 49 per cent or less does want a relationship. Whenever I voice this reality, I receive a barrage of objections. Of course, the person is 300 per cent convinced that all she wants in the world is a relationship. Huge amounts of energy and resources have been devoted to this end, and yet she is still single. Consciously, she does indeed desire a relationship but unconsciously the stronger desire is to stay single. Upon investigation, it may emerge that the last three times the person was in a relationship she was deeply hurt and rejected and in this case it is easy to understand why (unconsciously) she would avoid another one. Once again, until she is prepared to understand and embrace this, she will not change the current reality or set a different intention (conscious and unconscious.)

The following illustration is purposefully sensitive and controversial. Let us take an example of an attractive woman in her early 30s who is in an abusive relationship with a man. She is being physically hit on a regular basis. I have worked in a crisis centre for battered women and so I know and understand from difficult experience that it is extremely hard to persuade a woman to leave an abusive relationship. The statistics are overwhelming, showing that women consistently return to such a relationship and drop all charges. In the case where the man drops dead or moves out for good, the woman has an opportunity to be fully supported therapeutically and nurtured. During this period, she repeatedly maintains to her close friends that all she wants is to find a kind, supportive man. She wills this and intends this with the whole of her conscious mind. Once she has recuperated, she goes to a social event with over a hundred people present, where several men show great interest in her. The interest is not reciprocated and instead, she finds herself making a beeline for one particular man and starts dating him. Two months later, he physically abuses her for the first time. Devastated, she cannot believe her bad luck.

The unconscious mind is ingenious. She probably discovered the only male physical abuser at that event. Her unconscious antenna was entirely reliable. The reason that this example is so powerful is that unless and until the abused person, whether male or female, understands that he or she is unconsciously creating this situation, investigates why and hence takes responsibility for that truth, he or she is destined to repeat the toxic cycle. The second step is to understand how to reverse the seed of intention that has led to this outcome and how to create a happy and supportive relationship. The purpose of this book is to explain fully how we can reset our intention and plant a different seed.

As a seven- and eight-year-old boy, I was physically beaten several times a week by other boys in my school. Naturally, it was a particularly traumatic time in my life. Decades later, it is obvious to me that the seed of intention that led to my being bullied had been planted a lot earlier. By this age, I was already passive, over-sensitive and over-indulged. Arriving at an austere, all-male boarding school, I was a beacon of vulnerability for others' aggression. In truth, if any one of us travelled up and down the breadth of the country, visiting primary schools in their mid-morning break, and observed the children playing, it would soon become apparent which three or four schoolchildren were likely to be picked on and bullied. The dynamics of this are clearly present in both the recipient and the perpetrator. The sensitivity and vulnerability evident in some children attract the aggression of others. For various reasons, it is difficult for victims of abuse to understand the inconvenient truth that it is impossible to be a victim without an abuser. Equally, it is impossible to be an abuser without a victim. Hence, the world is full of victims looking for abusers and abusers looking for victims. Guess what? They find each other.

People will naturally rebel and revolt at this simple idea. A large part of the difficulty in recognizing this truth is that the wider community colludes with the unhealthy dynamic by berating the abuser and consoling the victim. While this seems entirely reasonable and understandable, it keeps both parties stuck. Of course, a number of different reasons or explanations may account for why an individual created this unconscious intention. For example, many girls who are physically and emotionally abused by a father repeat the pattern. Alternatively, a young woman who has been abused by a male figure on the periphery of the family or by a stranger may well find herself recreating this scenario. The logic of this hidden intention is that the compulsion to recreate a traumatic event is, in every situation, in part an unconscious desire to heal and move through the trauma. Sadly, this rarely occurs and the pattern goes on.

Since I had experienced intense physical bullying as a young child, my default pattern through life became 'victim', so I am familiar with this energetic dynamic. I attracted into my life people who were aggressive towards me or abused me in some way. My responses were passive aggressive behaviour, depression, shut down and withdrawal from life. Now that I have worked through this dynamic over a period of decades and taken responsibility for co-creating unhealthy relationships, I have arrived at a place in my life where I no longer find myself vulnerable to abuse. I would go so far as to say that it would not be

There is no possibility of fundamentally changing our life unless we accept responsibility for the reality we are currently creating.

possible for someone to bully me today; a perpetrator would not be drawn to me and would find someone else to abuse.

~

Each of these illustrations is designed to highlight two critical elements that we need to appreciate if we are to understand intention. The first is that there is no possibility of fundamentally changing our life or fulfilling our potential unless we accept responsibility for the reality we are currently creating. The great news about this approach is that if I am creating a particular scenario now – for example, an unhappy relationship – I can, equally, create a different scenario, a happy relationship. If I am stuck in a perception that life is happening to me and out of my control, I am like a cork bobbing on an ocean and can do nothing to change or reverse my fate. Moving beyond this passive and deluded state is a prerequisite to an understanding of the infinite power of intention.

Secondly, an understanding of how we consistently unconsciously create situations that are seemingly undesirable is necessary in order to change those aspects of our life that lead to frustration and misery. If we can accept and embrace these two simple principles, we can create the life that fulfils our dreams.

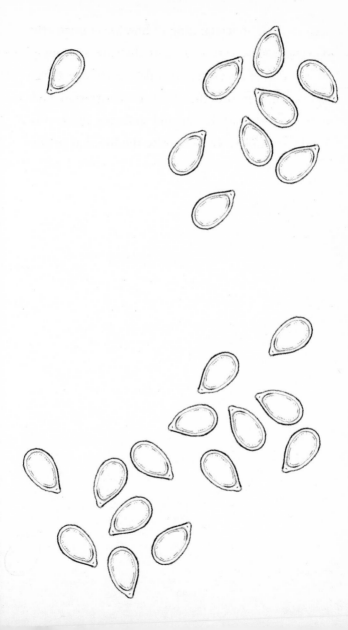

TWO

PLANTING

There are two aspects to planting: the seed and the soil. Neither a damaged seed planted in rich, fertile soil nor a healthy seed planted in poor-quality soil will flourish. It is critical to start out with a healthy, vibrant seed and good-quality, nutritious soil.

THE SEED

FIRSTLY, WE WILL focus on how to create the ideal seed of intention. It is not important to accept or acknowledge this but the truth is that we are not creating the seed of intention; we are discovering the seed within us and giving birth to it in an articulate and clear way.

A necessary condition for discovering our intention is to create a sense of space and stillness both in the outer world and in the inner world. It is very important that we allocate quality time when we are confident of not being disturbed. Once we have established this space and time, we need to undertake a process of putting down on paper (or on a screen, if your preference is digital) a flow of ideas. For some people this might be akin to a brainstorming session, others might be familiar with mind mapping or other similar tools.

CREATING SPACE

1 The best way to create space and stillness is to be in a new physical space. Get out of your office or your kitchen; go somewhere soothing to you. This could be a library, a church, in nature or in a quiet room in your house.

2 Ensure no mobile phone or other digital device can distract you.

3 Close your eyes, withdraw your attention from the outside and bring your awareness to your breathing and to the beat of your heart. Breathe deeply for 2 or 3 minutes.

The human brain is divided into two parts of equal size, frequently referred to as the left brain and the right brain. The left brain is rational, logical, analytical, task-oriented, problem solving, linear and masculine. It controls the right-hand side of our body. The right brain is intuitive, creative, magical, spontaneous, irrational, non-linear (spiral) and feminine. It controls the left-hand side of our body. Although these two parts of our brain are of equal dimension, we constantly live from our left brain, which is overused, while we neglect and ignore our right brain, which is underused. The process of discovering our intention is a right-brain activity and an opportunity to redress this imbalance. Therefore, before we start, it is important to centre the body and mind in order to find inner stillness and quiet from the relentless outer noise of daily life. Everyone has their own particular way of accessing this internal space and peace.

Whatever our preferred approach, we are allowing ideas and thoughts to bubble up inside and capturing these as they arise. It is often helpful to start with an open-ended question, such as: 'What do I want my life to look like five years from now?' Or 'What are

Everyone has
their own
particular way
of accessing this
internal space
and peace.

my priorities in the year ahead?' Or 'What do I most want to change about my life?'

This process has no time limit; there is no rush. You can always return to it on several occasions and add to, and refine, your thoughts and ideas. As you record the words, images and feelings that arise, certain key sentences or words will stand out. This often occurs by way of a resonance within the body, a feeling in the gut or the heart that affirms a particular aspect. Towards the end of each session, which might last anything from 30 minutes to 2 hours, stand back from the data that you have recorded and reflect upon patterns and the crucial phrases. It will become apparent which are the most important to you at this time. Carry on with these sessions until you feel the process is complete, and then you can hone your thoughts and ideas into four or five strong ingredients.

While I provide a number of examples on the following page, there is a caveat in that I do not want you to be too influenced by these. This whole process is about discovering your unique seed of intention. Many people, including myself, create two separate intentions. One is for my personal life and one is for my career. Alternatively, you can create one intention to embrace both aspects of your life. The choice is entirely yours and you do not need to make this choice until the end of the process, as the process itself might well guide you to a more definitive answer.

Example A

1 To buy a home
2 To travel more
3 To be calmer
4 To feel more secure about Stanley
5 To create space for family gatherings

These ingredients when put together create the following intention: 'To buy a house and travel more extensively while being calmer in my life, feeling more secure about Stanley and creating more space for family gatherings.'

Example B

1 To be more successful in my career
2 To buy a house on the Isle of Wight
3 To feel more fulfilled in my marriage
4 To spend more quality time with my family

These ingredients when put together create the following intention: 'To be more successful in my career, buy a house on the Isle of Wight, feel more fulfilled in my marriage and spend more quality time with my family.'

Example C

1 To establish a loving relationship with a partner
2 To achieve a healthy relationship with food
3 To change my job
4 To have £200,000 of savings

These ingredients when put together create the following intention: 'To establish a loving relationship with a partner, achieve a healthy relationship with food, change my job and have £200,000 of savings.'

At the time of writing this book, my own personal intentions are:

My personal life

1 To celebrate my life
2 To give up the stories of the past
3 To heal through a loving relationship with my beloved
4 To open my heart
5 To have it all

These ingredients when put together create the following intention: 'To celebrate my life, giving up the stories of the past, healing through a loving relationship with my beloved, opening my heart and having it all.'

My professional life

1 To create a global business
2 To provide financial value of £30 million
3 To transform businesses
4 To embody light-heartedness
5 To achieve recognition as a pioneer

These ingredients when put together create the following intention: 'To create a global business with a financial value of £30 million through transforming businesses, embodying light-heartedness and achieving recognition as a pioneer.'

The process of discovering our seed of intention is like finding out the ingredients for a cake. There are many varieties of cake and an infinite number of possible ingredients. However, most, but not all, cakes have certain ingredients in common. For example, the vast majority of cakes contain flour, although this might be plain, wholemeal, wheat or spelt. Equally, most cakes contain eggs but many delicious cakes contain no flour, eggs or refined sugar. It is the same with discovering our intention; there are some categories that the majority of us share – creating financial security, establishing wealth or financial resources are common. Likewise, establishing a romantic relationship is a frequent component whereas, for some people, none of these might be important.

The essential keys to this process are not to copy other examples (as on previous pages), to disregard other people's opinions, whether they are experts or not, and to be fully committed to discovering the inner mind-body seed that is particular to each of us. Just as each one of us has unique DNA, each one of us contains an individual intention that is waiting to be discovered.

In the preceding examples, you will notice that each and every intention starts with an active verb. It is important to express our intention in this way as this provides forward momentum and support for realizing it. It is also vital to be as specific as possible and to choose our words carefully. Our words and expressions should resonate with our mind body. For example, we could say that we want to create financial security but this expression is vague and means completely different things to different people. For one person, £50,000 and a house boat on the Thames might represent financial security whereas for another £5 million in the bank might not be sufficient. Hence, when you are connecting inside, it is important to discover precisely how much money you want to create and to articulate this within the intention. The same applies to the quality of the relationship you seek or the home you want to buy.

Just as each one
of us has unique
DNA, each one of
us contains an
individual intention
that is waiting to
be discovered.

Once we have arrived at the first draft of articulating our intention, we need to test and refine it. The way to do this is to write down each ingredient on a separate sheet of paper (A4 size works well) and then the whole intention on a final sheet. For example, if you have four ingredients, you end up with five pieces of paper, one for each ingredient and one for the whole. Lay all the pieces of paper on the floor in front of you in a random way. Step back to survey and reflect upon these for a moment or two. Select any one of the ingredients and step on to that piece of paper. It can be helpful, but it is not essential, to close your eyes when doing this. When you step on to the piece of paper, you are stepping into the energy or the essence of the words written on it. As you begin to relax into the essence of this particular ingredient, reflect upon the words and consider if any refinement or tweaking will bring a stronger resonance to your inner vibration.

To illustrate this, when I am undertaking this process with clients, I frequently find that a small nuance can create a big impact. For example, stepping into an articulated ingredient of intention that states 'being more artistic' might become 'to allow more creativity'. The latter creates greater connectivity within and the person experiences it as if an inner dial has moved from say a six to a nine. In another example, a stated intention that reads 'create a more loving relationship with my spouse' becomes 'creating deeper connection and intimacy with my wife'. The subtle difference is experienced in the body. During this process, the more attuned you can be to listening to your body, the greater the accuracy and impact of your intention.

The reason for this part of the process is that it is vital to engage with the body. All of us spend far too much of our lives absorbed with an inner dialogue in our minds. We all tend to live in our heads. The mind is full of delusions, distortions, distractions and pitfalls of every variety. In contrast, our body is a much more reliable source of our truth. By physically stepping on to the piece of paper and into the energy of the expression, we are allowing and inviting our body to reveal invaluable information. An intention is an inner impulse that arises from the

When we embody the intention, we are accessing a much greater part of ourselves and bringing the conscious and unconscious into harmony.

deep cellular memory of the body; it is akin to our own DNA.

In addition, we know about the power of the unconscious in supporting or undermining our intention. It has often been said that the body is the unconscious, and for me, there is a self-evident truth about this. Hence, when we embody the intention, we are accessing a much greater part of ourselves and bringing the conscious and unconscious into harmony.

Repeat the process of stepping on to the paper, listening to the body's response and refining the words accordingly. If necessary, as we undertake this process, we can explore the use of different words or expressions and re-test our body's reaction to them.

There is no rush. It is far better to take your time over a period of several weeks than to race through the process to get to an end result. We are not in a hurry to get to the end goal; we are creatively exploring and discovering a deeper truth about ourselves. It is similar to a careful, diligent archaeological dig.

Once we have gone through each ingredient in this way, it is time to step on to the piece of paper that contains the intention as a whole. Here, we ask two important questions. Firstly: 'Is there anything here that does not need to be here?' Allow time for this question to vibrate through your body. Trust the response to come from within, not from your mind. The second question is: 'Is there anything missing?' Again, allow time for this question to linger and permeate the cells of your body.

After this, create fresh pieces of paper with the refined ingredients and intention and repeat the whole exercise. If necessary, repeat it three or four times, although this is not often required.

In every case where I have undertaken this process personally or guided a client through it, there is a moment when the intention as a whole aligns with the energetic frequency of the mind body. For some people this feels like being 99 per cent accurate (or as close as we can get) whereas for others it feels like a complete fit – two jigsaw pieces slotting together. Once you are satisfied that you have discovered the truth of your intention to the best of your ability, you can create the final pieces of paper to keep. These might include the use of colour and/or images. If you can have each piece laminated, so much the better.

We have now discovered a healthy quality seed.

THE SOIL

PREPARATION OF HEALTHY nutritious soil is a far simpler process than discovering the seed. To use the analogy of baking a cake, it is similar to turning on the oven and waiting for it to heat up to the correct temperature. The soil into which we will plant our healthy seed is our own mind-body existence. There is nothing outside ourselves that will impact the quality of our soil. We will go into greater depth about how best to cultivate and maintain the quality of the soil in the next chapter. In the meantime, it is sufficient to understand that the preparation work includes being committed and allowing brief periods of space and quiet time for reflection, listening to our bodies, becoming more open, developing curiosity, becoming more spontaneous, affirming trust and valuing intuition and instinct.

The following meditation will initiate and support how to plant your healthy seed in fertile soil. Some people may like to follow the text on the following pages, others may prefer to use the audio version (see the Notes section on page 185 for where to find these meditations). If your seed of intention has four ingredients rather than five, you can adjust the meditation accordingly. Each ingredient is treated as a separate seed.

Intention Meditation

In your own time, close your eyes and begin the process of withdrawing attention from the outside and bringing awareness to the inside.

A beautifully simple way to support this is with the breath. So bring your awareness to the in-breath; the way in which you draw that breath into your body. With each in-breath bring a little more awareness to the way in which that breath enters your body.

Breath is life. The way that you breathe life into your body.

And when you are ready, bring an equal amount of awareness to the out-breath; the way in which you then return that breath to the atmosphere.

The breath comes in and the breath goes out. The tide comes in and the tide goes out.

And on an in-breath of your choosing, take a deep, long breath into your heart. Both your physical heart and your heart centre. Allow the breath to come up through the torso and take that breath deeply into your heart and continue with each and every breath to breathe deeply into your heart's centre.

With each in-breath allow your heart to expand. Both your physical heart and your heart centre are expanding with each in-breath.

On the out-breath invite your heart to open.

On the in-breath, your heart is expanding and growing; and on the out-breath your heart is opening, just like a flower to sunlight, opening to all that is in each moment.

On the in-breath expanding and on the out-breath opening.

And in a few moments time I am going to ask you to take an even deeper, longer breath into your heart.

Now is that moment – take a deep, deep breath into the centre of your heart and on the out-breath I want you to fall, fall right into the centre of your heart.

And as you arrive there notice the beautiful trees, the bright colours of the flowers, the wonderful scent in the air.

And you notice one big tree to your right with a bench underneath it and you wander over to the bench and sit there for a few moments admiring the beauty and the splendour of the garden of your heart in all its majesty. Breathe in the scent, the beauty and the tranquillity of this sacred place.

After a few moments, you stand up and walk over toyour right and you notice there an empty bed full of dark, nutritious soil. You wander over to the bed and kneel down on the grass and with your right hand you scoop up some of the soil, noticing the richness, the fertile nature of this earth.

And in your left hand you notice a small number of seeds, five or six, and these are the seeds that make up the ingredients of the intention you have discovered. So with your right hand, with your index finger, you now make a small hole in this rich, nutritious soil and then you take the first seed from your left hand. You don't need to remember exactly which intention the seed represents, but you take the seed, which is the first ingredient of your intention, and you gently place it in the small hole you've created. Then you tenderly fold the soil over the seed, smoothing over the top of the soil. And as you do so, you wish this seed well on its journey to fulfilling its innate potential.

When you are ready, with the index finger on your right hand, a foot or so to the right, you make another hole in the soil and lovingly you pick up the second seed, which is the second ingredient of your intention, and you place it in the hole you have created for it. Gently, softly you fold in the soil just like tucking a small child into bed, wishing this seed well on its journey through the night and knowing that it contains every-thing it needs to flower beautifully.

And when you're ready, you create a third hole with the index finger on your right hand and you take the third seed, the third ingredient of your intention, from your left hand and gently place it in the hole you have created, covering it, submitting it to the darkness of the soil, wishing it well, giving it your blessing as it begins its journey to fulfilling its potential.

In your own time, create a fourth hole and take the fourth seed, the fourth ingredient of your intention, and place it lovingly in the hole you have provided, gently covering it over, bidding it well on its journey to fulfilment. Again giving it your blessing.

And if there were four ingredients in your intention, the fifth and final seed will be the intention as a whole, so make a fifth hole. And if there were five ingredients in your intention then the fifth seed will be the final ingredient. Either way, place this seed in the special hole you have created, folding it up into the darkness of the soil, trusting that it contains everything it needs to grow to its full potential.

And if you have a final seed in your left hand, make a sixth hole and this will be your intention as a whole. You plant it in exactly the same way.

Kneeling on the grass, you see the surface of the soil; none of the seeds can be seen. They have begun their journey in darkness surrounded by this rich, fertile soil.

And as you stand up you notice to your right a watering can. Pick up the watering can and lovingly spray the earth, the area where your seeds are planted, providing these seeds with vital water, feeding the ingredients of your intention.

When you've finished, stand back and in your own way, in your own time, provide these seeds with your blessing in the knowledge, the trust and the confidence that each one of these seeds and your intention as a whole contains everything necessary to grow into a magnificent flower, to fulfil its potential.

When you've done this, in your own way make a commitment to visit the garden of your heart at least once a day to lovingly water and give your blessing to these small but robust seeds.

And with one final glance at the bed, walk back to the bench underneath the tree. Sit quietly for a moment and reflect on the special, sacred planting that you have just undertaken.

When you are ready, in your own time, slowly, gradually walk out of the garden of your heart and bring yourself back into the room wherever you are, and gently open your eyes.

THREE

SUNLIGHT
AND WATER

Now we have discovered the seed of our intention and planted it in the rich, fertile soil of our open-hearted commitment, we need to understand how to support and maintain it to encourage optimum growth. As well as nutritious soil, every seed needs sunlight and water in order for it to grow to its full potential. In terms of supporting this process, there are two serious pitfalls at either end of the spectrum. Firstly, we can neglect the seed and fail to provide it with sufficient sunlight or water. In such a case, the seed will perish before it even has a chance to sprout. We are all far too familiar with this pattern. How many times have we created an intention to lose weight, go to the gym, meditate daily, learn Spanish, never to get off the starting block?

An intention is a necessary condition for anything to come into existence. Nothing can exist without intention. However, it is not sufficient. Intention on its own will not guarantee an abundant harvest. There are certain additional requirements. At the other end of the spectrum we can overwater any seed or plant and this will drown the roots, so the plant will perish. More house plants die from overwatering than through underwatering. We have become accustomed to seeking to control events through increasing effort and willpower. This is consistent with our cultural norm; there is too much activity, too much frenetic thinking, too much noise. Having set an intention, we often set about over-thinking, over-worrying, seeking to control and becoming obsessed about our desired outcome.

When we plant a seed in the ground, for many weeks or months it remains out of sight, quietly germinating. We don't constantly visit the spot where we have planted it and fret about whether anything is happening. Neither do we dig up the soil to check that it is still there and to see if any growth has taken place. Equally, as it begins to

An intention is
a necessary
condition for
anything to come
into existence.
Nothing can exist
without intention.

sprout, we don't observe it 20 or 30 times a day and agitate over the apparent lack of visible movement. In contrast, many people act like this having created an intention. Their mental activity and preoccupation are completely disproportionate and actually get in the way, inhibiting the natural evolution of that intention.

> The best way to support and nourish a seed that you have planted in the ground is to water it daily and ensure it has sufficient light, in the sure knowledge that the seed contains everything it needs to grow into a magnificent plant. It is precisely the same with our own seed of intention.

At the end of the last chapter you were invited to undertake the intention guided meditation. This is a profound and symbolic process by which we plant the seed of intention and set it on its journey. The following two daily practices provide the ideal environment to maximize the potential growth of your seed, giving it sunlight and water.

Sunlight

Every morning, step on to your laminated intention for a maximum of two to three minutes. Build this practice into your morning routine so that it becomes a habit. Why is this so important? We have looked at the way in which the unconscious undermines our conscious intention. We have also noted that the body is the unconscious. By physically stepping on to and into our stated intention in this way at the beginning of each day, we are literally placing our intention in the cellular memory of our body. In common with all practices of this nature – yoga, meditation, a gym work-out – on some days we may find it empowering and energizing whereas on other days we will encounter great resistance and on still others we may find it boring. All of this is to be welcomed and we simply continue undertaking our routine. An important aspect of efficacy of outcome is showing up. As you commit to this practice, you will in turn learn a lot about your internal resistance to creating the reality you want. It fascinates me how so many of us don't or won't spend two or three minutes out of a 24-hour period – that is 0.2 per cent of each 24 hours – committing to ourselves in this way.

The reasons why we resist are varied. We may be embarrassed, we may have already decided that it will not work (we know better), we have not got time in the mornings and so on. The truth is that whatever the conscious reason we may give to ourselves, if we are not prepared to do something simple like this for two or three minutes each day, we are already resisting and undermining the intention that we maintain consciously that we want.

Water

The second daily practice necessary for the evolution of your seed is to visit the garden of your heart each evening after you have got into bed, before you go to sleep. This extremely relaxing and soothing process is particularly effective at this stage of the day, before you undergo the transition from conscious waking to

reparative sleep. Again, this is a two- or three-min-
ute practice and it is always revealing how many
people encounter resistance to doing it. Visiting
the garden is a powerfully symbolic way in which
to provide much-needed water to your growing and
expanding intention.

After a period of several days visiting the garden
of your heart, you will begin to see small sprouts
emerging from the soil. It is interesting and sometimes surprising how one or two shoots grow quicker
than the others. Over time, there can be significant
differences in the size and robustness of the evolving
plants. This is valuable information. Occasionally, a
particular seedling will wither and die. This merely
reflects unconscious resistance. In such circumstances, we simply plant a fresh seed for this element
of the intention and keep doing so until we have a
seed that grows strongly.

I once worked with a client who told me that on five
consecutive occasions when she went into the garden

Visiting the garden is a powerfully symbolic way in which to provide much-needed water to your growing and expanding intention.

of her heart, she discovered that a particular seedling she had planted was covered in gloss paint. This was quite dramatic. She kept re-planting a fresh seed for this aspect of her intention and seven months later this desired part came to be in a very beautiful, unusual way. I have been using this intention meditation for more than ten years and over that time numerous significant events have been created in my life with this support.

It is important to clarify that both the sunlight and water practices can be carried out at any time in the day, in a more ad hoc or spontaneous way, as a substitute for and in addition to the suggestions above. However, experience shows that creating a habit of a practice at the same time each day has added benefits. You are much more likely to do it every day and the repetition of doing it at the same time creates a more embedded experience.

Implicit in this middle way of avoiding neglect at one end of the spectrum and agitation at the other end, is having trust and confidence in the seed of intention itself. I often ask clients the question: 'Does an acorn know what it is to be an oak tree?' Or 'Does a pumpkin seed know what it is to be a pumpkin?' It seems to me that the answer is always 'Yes and no.' On the one hand, a seed does not have knowledge of what it can become in the way we understand knowing. However, an acorn does contain everything it needs to grow into a magnificent oak with a relatively modest amount of water and sunlight. We can stand back and have confidence in the ability of the acorn or seed to fulfil its potential.

It is exactly the same with our own seed of intention that we have carefully articulated. We do not need to make it happen, we do not need to control it, and we do not even need to know how it is going to happen. We need to cultivate the confidence and trust that it will happen in its own time. For example, if one element of our intention is to develop a loving, supportive relationship with a partner, we can foster inner trust and confidence that the ideal person will show up in our lives at the appropriate time. If we refuse all invitations to social events and don't leave the house, this lack of openness and willingness is akin to creating an intention and completely neglecting it. What is more common is to spend copious waking hours planning dinner parties and other social events, working out who in the room is 'the one', or fretting about why this person hasn't shown up yet and generally trying to control the process. This approach, like overwatering, actively inhibits the desired outcome and kills off the intention.

Intention is the DNA of all reality. In the human body, each one of us has approximately 75 trillion cells. It is extremely difficult for us to imagine one trillion, let alone 75 trillion, but each individual cell contains what it is to be us. It carries the blueprint of who we are. According to Dr Deepak Chopra, every cell in our body has a higher purpose in so far as it is interested in the whole rather than the individual. The cells in the stomach are not concerned just with the stomach but are also digesting food, supporting the brain and the functioning of the body as a whole. Equally, the cells in the brain are not concerned with the brain only but with coordinating the legs and arms as well as many other processes in the body.

In addition to being interested in the whole, every cell operates through the principle of efficiency – do less and accomplish more.

This aspect of alignment owes its roots to a theme running through Western civilization, which pairs the concepts of the macrocosm and the microcosm – human beings (microcosm) parallel the whole universe (macrocosm) and vice versa, a view also known as 'the macrocosm is the microcosm'. This view was most fully developed by the early Greek philosophers, especially Plato in one of his dialogues, *Timaeus*. It arises from the observation that there is a similarity in pattern, nature and structure between human beings and the universe. This approach incorporates within it the idea that the microcosm contains the memory of the whole, just as the individual cell carries the memory of the whole person.

Intention is the
DNA of all reality.

Every cell is extremely adept at giving and receiving from other cells. Our cells naturally create an environment of support and alignment; this is interdependency. In all human relationships there are only three ways of relating. It is the same for the cells in our body and our own relationship towards our seed of intention. The first is based on dependency, an unhealthy dynamic based on neediness. The mantra of a dependent relationship is: 'Please don't leave me. I will die.' Neediness is correlated with anxiety and abandonment. If we are overly dependent towards our intention, we will suffocate it in exactly the same way that a needy person in a relationship suffocates the person he or she professes to love.

The second dynamic is independence. This is also an unhealthy mode of being in a relationship, based on detachment and disconnection (often compensating for a fear of commitment or intimacy). The battlecry is: 'I don't need you.' This is correlated with aloofness, arrogance and control. If we are independent in relation to our intention, we are detached and disconnected, merely going through the motions, just as in a relationship if we are completely independent, there is no possibility of intimate connection and our partner will eventually find this elsewhere.

The third dynamic is interdependence. This is highly desirable and satisfying for both parties. It is based on the spirit of partnership – 'We are in this together' – and a mutuality of respect and need established upon recognition of the whole. Any relationship involves three entities – the two individuals and the relationship itself. Often, when there is conflict or a power struggle between the two principal parties, an easy solution is to put the relationship first and ask, 'What is most needed for the relationship right now?' I use this regularly in couples therapy because it enables the individuals to loosen their grip on their (defended) position and move forward. By creating a higher purpose or bigger picture the relationship dynamic can continue to evolve in a loving direction. It is exactly the same in relation to our seed of intention. Understanding that the seed of intention already has within it a memory of the whole (just as the acorn knows how to become an oak) allows us to trust in confidence that the intention will naturally fulfil its role. We in turn will play our part by making choices that support our intention, thereby creating an inter-dependent relationship.

Interdependence is the natural and normative way in which an individual cell in our body relates to the organism as a whole. Intention has the same dimension of being embedded in the DNA of the individual cell while at the same time containing the big picture or vision of what is possible. According to Dr Deepak Chopra, when an individual cell loses the memory of wholeness, we have a disease. A cancer cell is a cell that has lost its memory of wholeness. The cell is operating on an 'only for me' basis. In this state of selfishness, it attacks other cells and starts to destroy the body. Its integrity and existence are interdependent upon every other cell in the body but it does not recognize this. It pursues its own agenda to the cost and detriment of the whole – it develops independence.

In addition to the daily sunlight and water practices set out on pages 66–9, nurturing our seed of intention requires us to think and act in support of it and have confidence and trust that our seed will do the rest. Just as in order to keep our bodies healthy, we need to make decisions that reinforce the concept of health – exercise, eating, rest and wellbeing practices – we need to learn to align our thinking and actions with our intention. In this way, our intention, as well as being the DNA of what we are seeking to create, becomes a guiding light or compass in informing our decision making. In our daily life, whether at home or at work, when we encounter dilemmas or straight-forward decisions, we can ask: 'Does this support our intention or not?' This question becomes a brilliant device for working through the jungle of life.

For example, if one element of your intention is to spend more quality family time and you are constantly being asked to attend business dinners or make trips abroad, it is extremely helpful to question whether this supports your intention. I am not advocating refusing to attend any business dinners or foreign work commitments but making the point that if you do not apply this principle some of the time, you are neglecting rather than supporting your articulated

It is natural and
to be expected
that when we
create a specific
intention,
resistance to it
will be both equal
and opposite.

intention, which is presumably important to you. There is a certain daily discipline and commitment to aligning with the intention that will create the life you want. If you just created an intention and then did nothing to support its fruition, of course it is not going to flower.

One further aspect of providing sunlight and water for the development of our intention is important. All of us operate within the physical universe, which means we are subject to certain laws and forces of nature. These forces, such as gravity and magnetism, are not up for debate. They are a given of our existence and have consequences, one of which is Sir Isaac Newton's third law of motion that for every action there is an equal and opposite reaction. It cannot be otherwise. Against this background, it is natural and to be expected that when we create a specific intention, resistance to it will be both equal and opposite. In my experience this is not well enough understood and so it undermines and erodes the fulfilment of our aspirations and dreams.

If we decide to have faith in something and at the first hurdle doubt arises, we often conclude that the faith was misplaced and give up. In contrast, if we understood that each time we express faith in something, we can expect to feel doubt as a natural and inevitable consequence, we can allow that doubt to be present in order to push through to the next level of aligning the intention. What tends to happen in practice is we often ignore, disregard or repress the doubt and as a result it becomes more potent and eventually impacts us in a more dramatic way. Alternatively, we find ourselves seduced into the doubt and attach to it in a negative way, convincing ourselves that our intention was fanciful and was never going to come to fruition anyway.

This is a mirror of the two pitfalls identified at the outset of this chapter. We either neglect (deny) the resistance or we indulge (agitate) it. The balanced approach is calmly and persistently to *recognize* the two opposing forces and to continue to sustain our seed of intention through commitment and daily discipline and thus to stand firm with our intention.

DEVELOPING TRUST

Developing trust is a
repeating cycle. We need
to continue to integrate
until we get to the ultimate
synthesis, which we may
never reach...

Continuous evolution

Integration

LEVEL 3

The re-reaction is
moving to a higher
level of trust

SYNTHESIS
(TRUST) → DOUBT

Integration

LEVEL 2

The re-reaction is
moving to a higher
level of trust

SYNTHESIS
(TRUST) → DOUBT

Integration

LEVEL 1

START

TRUST → DOUBT

Inner Knowing Meditation

(See page 185 for links to audio versions of the meditations.)

When you are ready, begin the process of withdrawing your attention from the outside and bringing awareness to the inside.

Bring awareness to the body, to the breath, simply becoming more and more aware of the physicality of your body. We can rest inside in the knowledge that we have discovered a clarity of intention.

And we have embodied, we have aligned this intention through watering and sunlight. Having discovered the seed of intention, and created alignment with the Universe, in this moment there is nothing to do. In this moment there is nowhere to go, nothing to do, just breathing, relaxing in awareness of your body.

As you rest in your body, allow your awareness to drift up to the left-hand side of your brain. With each breath bring a little more awareness to the left-hand side of your brain. This is the part of your body that is rational, logical, analytical; it's busy, it's doing, it's frenetic. It is in control and driving the process.

Just take a moment to be more aware of the tremendous effort generated by this side of your brain, thinking, analysing, working everything out, each moment of the waking day. We need our rationality, we need our clear thinking. Take a moment to honour this overworked, overused function of the body.

And our left brain can help with the process of integrating the shadow of our intention. As a positive element of our attention arises, there is a reaction, equal and opposite. And here in the left brain we can welcome the shadow, we can integrate the opposite, and we can go to a new level of affirming our intention.

Now, when you are ready, create a shift in your awareness from the left-hand side to the right-hand side. It might take you a few moments to really encourage and support this movement away from the overactive left-hand side of your brain. But keep bringing your awareness to the right-hand side.

This is the area of creative, magical, intuitive knowing. It is not linear, it operates in a spiral. This is the place of wisdom; it is the place that doesn't need to make sense. It is not rational. Just feel the way in which this kind of knowing has permission to dance, permission to think outside the box. To think and say things that don't make sense, that don't add up. This is the source of creativity, the source of wisdom.

Take a moment to rest and enjoy this infinite supply of creativity. Reflect on all those beautiful 'Aha' moments when thoughts arose we knew not where from. Maybe this area of your body has been neglected a little bit; maybe it's underused and inactive.

Take a moment to immerse yourself in the potentiality of the magical knowing that is available to you 24 hours a day, 7 days a week.

Take a moment to hold these two parts of your brain together like the integrated whole that it is; one supporting the other, the yin and the yang.

And when you're ready, take a deep, deep breath and on the out-breath I want you to fall through your body, fall through your chest, keep falling down through your stomach all the way into your gut and take a moment to breathe deeply into your belly.

Bring your awareness to this area of your body. In recent times much more interest in our gut is being generated. It's being acknowledged that our gut is probably more responsible for our mood than our brain, either the right- or the left-hand side.

A healthy gut creates a healthy mind, which creates a healthy organism. Breathe deeply into the energy of your gut and reflect for a moment on those times when you trusted your gut instinct. Important times in your life when your gut spoke and you listened.

We have become unconditioned to trusting our gut, to listening to the wisdom of our gut, and we need to re-learn, to re-practise accessing this vital wisdom. Breathe deeply into the energy of your gut and reflect now on those times when you have ignored this deep inner knowing, when you have overruled what your gut was trying to tell you and the consequences have not been so great.

All animal species rely on their gut instinct for survival and to thrive. Take a moment to recommit to learning more about this important area of knowing.

And when you're ready, take a deep breath and on the out-breath begin to move your awareness up from your gut, up your torso and into the centre of your chest.

Take a deep breath into your heart, continuing with each breath to breathe deeply into both your physical heart and your heart centre. On the in-breath allow your heart to expand and grow. On the out-breath invite your heart to open.

On the in-breath expanding and on the out-breath opening. In a moment I am going to ask you to take a deeper, longer breath into the centre of your heart.

Now is that moment. Take a deep, deep breath and on the out-breath I want you to fall deeply into the inner heart, keep falling, falling, falling into the inner heart.

With each breath allow yourself to fall deeper into your inner heart. This is a knowing beyond reason. As you fall more deeply into your inner heart there might be a feeling of space, of stillness, even a feeling of darkness. Just allow yourself to be still.

And as you rest in the centre of your heart, in this knowing beyond reason, beyond instinct, beyond intuition, picture the seed of your intention, not necessarily the words, just the essence, the energy of your intention.

From this place of deep inner knowing, become aware of the potential for growth, the magnificence of this seed of intention that you have discovered deep within yourself.

And bring awareness to the truth, that you have the inner power, the inner resources to create this reality from this place of rest, this place of non-doing.

From the centre of your heart, from this place of deep connection, you are aligned with the source of all creativity. You can picture the life that you choose to create, the full potential of your intention and know that it is there waiting to come to you.

Rest, in this deep inner knowing, with confidence, with curiosity, there's nothing to do, nowhere to go.

And in a few moments time I'm going to invite you to bring your attention back to the outer world and when you do that this deep inner knowing will withdraw into the background, but it will still be there, still sending out its signal to attract the intention you've articulated.

You can visit this place of deep knowing, beyond reason, any time you choose, night or day.

So in your own time, very slowly, very gradually bring your attention back to the room where you are.

Once we have discovered our seed of intention, planted it in rich, fertile soil and provided sunlight and water, we need to turn our attention to what gets in the way of it flowering to its full potential. As every gardener knows, however good the quality of the soil with which you start out, weeds will appear and begin to choke the plant. If weeding is carried out on a regular basis, the weeds never get a hold, so there is no damage. However, if they are allowed to build up, apart from being unsightly, they draw much-needed nutrition and energy away from the plant and may eventually overpower it. It is precisely the same with our seed of intention and the way in which human beings operate in the world.

We have already seen that once an intention has been fully articulated, it is inevitable and to be expected that an opposing force will arise (Sir Isaac Newton's third law of motion, see page 81). Within various spiritual traditions, this is often expressed as the universe 'testing us', that is to say we create a positive intention only to find that, within hours or days, we are seriously challenged and confronted by an obstacle to it. In my own experience, and also working with others, this is an extremely common phenomenon. I am suggesting that it is normal and inevitable. In the same way, having planted a seed, irrespective of the quality of the soil, weeds will arise. When this happens, it is easy to become discouraged and to give up. However, our role in such circumstances is simply to acknowledge the obstacle and re-affirm the intention.

The greatest threat to our conscious intention is what lies outside of our awareness – our unconscious. Just as weeds germinate and strengthen under the surface and out of sight, our intention is being undermined without our knowledge or awareness. The unconscious is frequently referred to as the shadow. Every living individual has a shadow that impedes and sabotages the life he or she is seeking to create, as illustrated in Chapter One in the analogy of the iceberg. The part of the iceberg under water is enormous compared with the part that we can see. It is the same with the depth of the earth compared with the visible surface. This also applies to our mind and conscious state. The vast area of our mind outside of awareness, in which potential weeds are lurking, is multi-layered and consists of five different levels.

Level 1 – The Perceptual Field

The basic division of awareness within human beings is referred to as the perceptual field. It has been suggested that each human being receives the same amount of data every day that Shakespeare received in his entire lifetime. I have no idea whether this is true but none of us need reminding of the constant bombardment of data that we now receive in modern life. It is little wonder that the bulk of this information is sent to the unconscious mind to be buried in nanoseconds.

Every time we walk down a busy street certain information is filtered through our senses. We take in sights, sounds and smells but the majority of this data is directed straight to the unconscious and stored outside of our awareness.

We all live our lives and interact with each other on the assumption (pretence) that there is one reality. I call this 'mono-dimensional reality'. In one sense, this is an extraordinary assumption because it is manifestly and self-evidently not true. Each one of us operates with an internal filter through which all experience passes. That filter is created, refined and moulded through our early family experience, our education, our culture and many other variables. We also operate an internal projector with which to apply our particular subjective concepts, structures, biases and prejudices to immediate experience. Hence, five people witnessing the same event, whether it is a car accident, a theatre play or an

Each one of us
operates with
an internal filter
through which
all experience
passes.

argument in the street, all have a different reality. This is because there is no one shared reality, yet we all assume and operate as if there is. Anyone who has ever been in an intimate relationship will discover the harsh truth of this fairly quickly. It can be clearly seen from these examples that information highlighted in the perceptual field of others is absent from our own and outside of awareness. This is true for all of us all the time.

Level 2 – The Personal

The data being divided between the conscious and the unconscious in a matter of nanoseconds, referred to earlier, is relatively neutral or unimpactful in terms of the selection criteria. Level 2 refers to information that poses a threat to our conscious identity. For this reason, it is consigned to the recycle bin of our mind (the unconscious) without our awareness. For example, we might be walking down a street and someone coming from the opposite direction reminds us of our father who was particularly difficult and domineering, so we immediately block that information and pretend to ourselves that the person doesn't exist. Equally, it is a regular occurrence for us to be having a conversation with a friend or acquaintance who says something that we don't want to hear, so we literally don't. We filter it out of our perceptual field because of its perceived threat. (It is important to acknowledge that alongside these experiences, which are many and varied, it is also true that at the other end of the spectrum, we often latch on to the perceived threat and obsess about it in our conscious mind. However, here we are concerned with the other end of the polarity.)

In addition to the above examples, which are perceived threats from the outside, we are daily confronted with perceived threats from within. Each one of us has created an identity, carefully crafting it over many decades, and we become convinced that this is who we are. We are attached to this version of ourselves. For example, we might have invested a lot of time and energy in seeing ourselves as kind, charming and honest. We reinforce this identity all the time. This is regularly referred to as our persona, which comes from a Greek word meaning a mask. When a thought or feeling arises within us that is not consistent with our identity, let's say a particularly nasty thought, we do not allow ourselves to acknowledge it. The nasty thought does not cease to exist but is immediately filed in a locked room in our unconscious mind. This process is going on within each one of us every minute of every day of our lives. It is equally true that if our identity is built around being aggressive and domineering to keep people away from us, then any tender or kind thought will be unacknowledged and confined to the basement.

We can begin to see how what is rejected lurks beneath the surface and one day will come back to bite us. A classic example of how this information is more powerful outside of awareness than if we had been able to integrate it is illustrated by the extraordinary number of priests in the Christian tradition who have been convicted of sexually abusing young children. In North America alone 23,000 priests have been convicted of such offences. This is the tip of the iceberg. It is critically important to understand that

When a thought
or feeling arises
within us that is
not consistent
with our identity,
we do not allow
ourselves to
acknowledge it.

the overwhelming majority of these men entered this vocation with a noble intention, genuinely wanting to serve their community and their Church. Over many years they asserted their positive or spiritual values and were not able to acknowledge or integrate shadow values that conflicted with them. The more the perceived negative values are repressed, the stronger they become. Eventually, both the priests and of course their victims pay a devastating price for this.

There are many other examples of such repression – the pacifist who has a burst of aggression, a rigid food fascist who suddenly finds himself gorging on a major sugar binge or a devout religious person who loses all faith and becomes an atheist. Where the identity is extremely strong and the conscious censor is impenetrable, the build-up of rejected data in the unconscious reveals itself in the body because the body is the unconscious. All physical illness and disease contains valuable messages for what it is that we need to acknowledge and integrate.

> Anything that we exclude due to a perceived threat, external or internal, becomes increasingly powerful, just like a weed out of control in our garden.

Level 3 – The Big Threat

Beyond and beneath the two levels of the perceptual field and the persona is the third level of the shadow, which consists of big-ticket and big-picture issues. Anyone who is in a relationship or has been in a relationship knows that at any given time a number of issues lie under the surface that are not being addressed. For example, in a heterosexual marriage during which the man has one or more affairs, the wife may not consciously know about them, but it is always the case that inwardly and unconsciously she does. From my clinical practice, I know that this scenario can continue for many years. The information is deliberately not allowed into awareness because the risk of addressing it threatens to destroy the marriage. For many individuals, this is too high a cost to pay. During my work as a therapist over many decades, I have seen many men and women who are shocked and devastated to discover a spouse or partner has had an affair lasting for several years. However, there is always an 'a-ha' moment when they eventually acknowledge to themselves (and to me) that they had always known yet chose to repress it.

There are, of course, less potentially explosive situations that remain hidden within relationships. The reason for not addressing situations is that they are perceived as threatening to the overall stability and structure of life. If these areas are allowed to expand and fester, the relationship itself does become threatened because there is less and less connection and intimacy. This is wonderfully illustrated by the following passage from *A Visit From the Goon Squad*, a work of fiction by Jennifer Egan.

> *Yet each disappointment Ted felt in his wife, each incremental deflation, was accompanied by a seizure of guilt; many years ago, he had taken the passion he*

*felt for Susan and folded it in half, so he no longer
had a drowning, helpless feeling when he glimpsed
her beside him in bed; her ropy arms and soft, gener-
ous ass. Then he'd folded it in half again so when
he felt desire for Susan, it no longer brought with it
an edgy terror of never being satisfied. Then in half
again, so that feeling desire entailed no immediate
need to act. Then in half again, so he hardly felt it.
His desire was so small in the end that Ted could slip
it inside his desk or a pocket and forget about it, and
this gave a feeling of safety and accomplishment of
having dismantled a perilous apparatus that might
have crushed them both. Susan was baffled at first,
then distraught; she'd hit him twice across the face;
she'd run from the house in a thunderstorm and
slept in a motel; she'd wrestled Ted to the bedroom
floor in a pair of black crotchless underpants. But
eventually a sort of amnesia had overtaken Susan;
her rebellion and hurt had melted away, deliquesced
into a sweet, eternal sunniness that was terrible in
the way that life would be terrible, Ted supposed,
without death to give it gravitas and shape. He'd
presumed at first that her relentless cheer was
mocking, another phase in her rebellion, until it*

came to him that Susan had forgotten how things
were between them before Ted began to fold up his
desire; she'd forgotten and was happy – had never
not been happy – and while all of this bolstered his
awe at the gymnastic adaptability of the human
mind, it also made him feel that his wife had been
brainwashed. By him.

The brilliance of this piece is that when Ted felt
authentic desire for his wife, it evoked in him a terror
of never being satisfied – a feeling he couldn't allow
himself to experience. He keeps shutting off and
although his desire shrivels, it seems preferable to
any pain he may otherwise have to face, giving him
an erroneous sense of safety. The idea that Ted and
Susan have 'dismantled a perilous apparatus that
might have crushed them both' is genius, because all
of us are convinced we wouldn't survive an encounter
with what we have repressed, let alone the battle-
ground of engaging with our partner's unconscious
baggage. Susan ends up denying her dreams for a
marriage of passion and partnership, and buries them
in her day-to-day routine of faux cheeriness. She has
to convince herself that she is happy in her marriage,

as facing the truth of her disappointment, along with the loss of her romantic dream, would be too much to bear. Like so many married women (and men) she soldiers on with daily life, increasingly disengaged from her true feelings, deaf to the call of her inner scream.

Big-ticket and big-picture issues equally apply to areas other than intimate relationships, for example work scenarios, family situations and illnesses. Even if we are fairly disciplined with our weed management and set time aside on a regular basis for addressing unspoken and unwelcome dynamics, this level of unarticulated, unseen shadow always persists.

Level 4 – The Legacy

It used to be fashionable to think that babies were innocent creatures born into this world with a *tabula rasa*, a blank slate. Based on such a view, an individual's character, personality traits and identity developed through the conditioning of environment, family, education, religious community and wider cultural influences. Hence the Jesuits maintained, 'Give me a boy until he is seven and he is mine for life.' However, over the last 60 years or so, a growing body of research and knowledge has revealed the amount of data and baggage with which we arrive. Each one of us has two separate ancestral lines at birth. The matrilineal line consists of our mother, her mother, her grandmother, her great grandmother and so on. The patrilineal ancestral line consists of our father, his father, his grandfather, his great grandfather and so on.

Several years ago, scientists were excited because they discovered that individual characteristics are carried across seven generations. Yogis in southeast Asia have maintained this for the last six thousand years. The research project worked with mice because the brain and DNA of mice are 98 per cent similar to humans. An aversion to the smell of cherry was created in an adult female mouse. Every time the smell of cherry was introduced to the mouse's environment, the mouse displayed symptoms of anxiety and stress, eventually becoming frenetic and hysterical. The mouse then gave birth to a litter, a female was selected and kept in a controlled environment in which there was no possibility of being exposed to the smell of cherry. The same process was repeated for one of her offspring and so on for a total of seven generations. The female mouse selected from the seventh generation was exposed to the smell of cherry and displayed the same level of symptoms as her ancestor. The information about the aversion is carried by the DNA for seven generations.

We are now much more familiar with the idea that the patterns and dysfunctions of our ancestors reveal themselves in us as we mature. Any particularly severe mental or emotional disturbance is always, in my experience, multi-generational. From a higher perspective, it is my view that each one of us incarnates in a particular lifetime for the main purpose of tidying up and healing the ancestral line. This is sometimes referred to as a soul contract. A simpler explanation is that this is merely evolution. Just as I resolve the unfinished business of my parents and grandparents, I pass down to my children those areas that I have not got around to prior to their arrival.

It is my view
that each one of
us incarnates in
a particular
lifetime for the
main purpose of
tidying up and
healing the
ancestral line.

Another objection to the blank canvas, which is far more controversial, is the notion that each one of us has lived many previous lifetimes. A significant minority of people living on our planet, maybe around 20 per cent, make sense of their lives through the idea and experience that each lifetime is simply part of a much longer journey. While I appreciate that given our perceptual field, we all tend to see what we are looking for and ignore what we are not seeking, my clinical work over 35 years has led me to believe that this is an intricate part of the evolution of our species and the evolution of our own individual soul. Each lifetime provides us with lessons necessary for our growth. If this position is true, which it may or may not be, it is another layer of shadow, which sits alongside our ancestral lines.

Level 5 – The Culture

Each one of us is born into a particular culture. In some countries, many different cultures operate. However, broadly speaking, each country and each culture has defining characteristics, which impact greatly on those who grow up within them. For example, it is impossible to understand the United Kingdom without an appreciation of the deeply embedded class system. In the United Kingdom, there are particular attitudes towards money, which stem from the British aristocracy and a system of elitism that views money as uncouth; status is far more important than wealth. In contrast, North America (although this is a country with widely different cultures) does not have this split attitude to money. The more successful you are and the more wealth you have, the more accepted you are.

In Asian countries, it is culturally normative that daughters grow up with the primary responsibility to look after their parents. It is regularly the case that women sacrifice the opportunity of a family of their own to be full-time carers of elderly parents. In the West, this is far less likely. In many cultures around the world, women still operate as second-class citizens and are essentially there to serve men, whereas in other cultures, a meaningful although partial liberation allows equality to be more the norm. These cultural influences are present at birth and shape the conscious and unconscious mind throughout each lifetime. If these influences are left unchecked and unchallenged, they will severely limit the potential of an individual in the same way that weeds will clog the growth of a healthy plant.

～

All of these levels of the unconscious are affecting our seed of intention and contain potential obstacles to its realization. For example, if an element of our intention is to achieve financial security and within our ancestral line several generations lived with a serious lack around money, this demon will persistently raise its head to undermine the stated intention. It can readily be seen that a correlation exists between the ancestral reality and the articulated intention. We are far more likely to long for financial security if we are carrying a multi-generational anxiety and fear that there will not be enough. This is where daily or weekly care and maintenance is required.

An example of level 2, personal threat, might be an individual who was put into foster care at the age of three. At the age of 37, one ingredient of her intention is to create emotional and physical security. Again, it is easy to see how this might be a longed-for aspiration. Her filter and projector will consistently throw up the threat of rejection and abandonment, which runs counter to her seed of intention. She will need to work through this in a diligent way.

In level 3, the big threat, if rather than folding the envelope, we have the courage to confront and address the issue from a position of being committed to working it through and staying within the relationship, then a feeling of liberation will be the outcome. There will be a sense of new energy, deeper connection and intimacy and both parties will fulfil more of their potential in the immediate aftermath.

I am aware that the accounts of the various levels of the unconscious, all of which contain potential threats – weeds – to the fulfilment of our intention, might seem overwhelming and impossible to redress. However, it is important to appreciate fully that we have started out with a quality seed, which we have planted in high-grade soil. Also, these various levels of threat do not need to be addressed all at once. A slow, disciplined commitment to recognizing and clearing these over a period of time is sufficient. The key, in each case, is awareness. We cannot change something or integrate something unless we have an awareness of it. All of the data referred to in levels 1, 2 and 3 begin life outside of awareness, just as the weed germinates below the surface of the soil. When it surfaces, we can pluck it out very easily. It is the same with each of these areas, all of which have the capacity to damage or stunt the growth of our potential.

Any process of change requires and follows three simple elements. The first is AWARENESS. As we have seen, without awareness of a particular issue or problem, it is impossible to do anything about it. Having allowed something into our conscious mind from the unconscious, i.e. awareness, we need to make a DECISION. I sometimes call it an existential decision. The decision to change is embedded in our seed of intention once articulated. The third element is DISCIPLINE. Once we have the awareness and

We cannot
change something
or integrate
something unless
we have an
awareness of it.

we have made the decision, we need to develop a daily discipline to move forward. None of this is achieved in a day. There is no quick fix. It is an iterative process that takes time. We do not have to deal with all of the obstacles at once. Just as the seed takes time to reach its full potential and weeding is a regular practice, so it is with ensuring that our intention achieves its abundant harvest.

Step 1: AWARENESS

Step 2: DECISION

Step 3: DISCIPLINE

Our seed has been planted. We are confident that it is receiving sufficient sunlight and water, and regular weeding is taking place. We now need to understand the importance of flow. Nature is a wonderful teacher. We are surrounded every day of our lives by constant reminders that everything in nature is in flow. The leaves grow on the trees, mature, fall to the ground and become compost before a new cycle begins. The oceans on the planet ebb and flow; the diurnal tide comes in and recedes twice a day, caused by slight variations in gravitational attraction between the earth and the moon and the sun in geometric relationship with locations on the earth's surface. As you are reading this, the earth is travelling around the sun at a speed of 67,000 miles per hour. All the planets in our solar system are in a constant state of movement.

In the same way, every human being is an embodiment of many systems. We, too, are in a constant state of flow. We have a cardiovascular and circulatory system that sends blood around the body via the heart, arteries and veins, delivering oxygen and nutrients to organs and cells. We have a digestive and excretory system that provides nutrients via the stomach and intestines and eliminates waste from the body. We have an endocrine system that provides chemical communications throughout the body using hormones. We have an autonomic nervous system (comprising the parasympathetic and the sympathetic nervous systems) that collects and processes information from the senses via nerves and the brain and tells our muscles to contract and relax, creating physical actions. We have several more systems including but not limited to the integumentary system (skin, hair, nails, glands and nerves), exocrine system, lymphatic system, immune system, reproductive system and respiratory system.

My favourite analogy for human beings is that we are like a river. When a river is flowing freely, it is healthy, vibrant and full of vitality. It creates an ecosystem where everything is interdependent. We have already noted the desirability of interdependency (see page 77). However, if a river gets blocked for any reason, it stagnates and becomes toxic very quickly. It is the same with us. All physical illness and somatic symptoms are in some essential way an impediment to the natural flow in our bodies. All of my work with individuals and businesses is about removing blocks in order to create greater flow. Given the constant flow in the outer world and the inner world, it is reasonable to conclude that optimum flow is the natural and healthy way of being. To support the realization of our intention, we must consider the following five separate areas of flow.

1. Physical

It is critical to take care of our physical self to ensure optimum flow (health). We need a balance of exercise, healthy diet, quality sleep, nurturing and being connected with nature. It astonishes me how so many people take very little care of their physical health. In many cases their bodies are screaming out for respite. If people are not taking care of their bodies, it usually follows that they are not taking care of themselves in other areas of life.

Both Chinese medicine, which is espoused by approximately two billion people, and Ayurvedic medicine, which caters for approximately one billion people, are rooted in and aligned with nature. According to traditional Chinese belief, humans are interconnected with nature and affected by its forces. The human body is seen as an organic whole in which the organs, tissues and other parts have distinct functions but are all interdependent on each other and on nature. The term Ayurveda combines the Sanskrit words *ayur* (life) and *veda* (science or knowledge). Ayurvedic medicine, as practised in India, is one of the oldest systems of medicine in the world. Many Ayurvedic practices pre-date written records and were handed down by word of mouth. The key concepts of Ayurvedic medicine include an understanding of universal interconnectedness (among human beings, their health and nature) and the body's constitution *(prakriti)* and life forces *(dosha)*, which are often compared to the four biologic humors of the ancient Greek system (Hippocratic medicine). We are part of and intrinsically aligned with nature, and all treatments recognize this.

Traditional Chinese medicine and Ayurvedic medicine both work within and alongside nature to restore the physical self to a state of wellbeing. The human body is probably the most sophisticated self-healing organism that has ever been created. In contrast, allopathic medicine, as practised in the West, treats symptoms rather than causes. It seeks to repress the symptom through synthetic drugs. What is repressed grows stronger until it eventually comes back in another form. A significant minority of scientists and doctors now recognize that the overuse of antibiotics (which repress symptoms) will inevitably give rise to a 'superbug' that is immune to all medicine and will wipe out huge numbers of people. Unless you address the underlying causes that give rise to the symptom, the problem will not go away.

In addition to our physical body, we all live and work in a physical space. Some homes are extraordinarily cluttered with boxes piled high, cupboards crammed with clothes that are never worn and objects everywhere. There is no natural energetic flow through the physical environment. It is the same with office space. Some offices I have visited have files piled precariously high, filing cabinets bulging with content,

Unless you address the underlying causes that give rise to the symptom, the problem will not go away.

desks covered with papers, all of which creates a heavy atmosphere. Offices can resemble a battery farm with endless rows of desks and tiny cubicles to work in. In the Eastern tradition, great importance is placed on feng shui – the natural flow of energy through a physical space. Feng shui is a system for arranging our surroundings in harmony and balance. In Chinese the words *feng* and *shui* mean wind and water, both of which flow in abundance around our planet.

Over the past 50 years or so, feng shui has gained momentum in the Western world, in the corporate environment as well as in our homes. In order to create an environment that supports realizing the full potential of our intention, it is helpful to undertake a regular decluttering of our professional and personal space. In recent times, the KonMari method has swept our shores to become extremely fashionable. Marie Kondo is a Japanese organizing consultant, who is evangelical about her methods and how they transform people's lives. Her method is based upon tidying up and her original Japanese art of decluttering and organizing has set off a decluttering craze across the globe.

How you create flow in your physical environment and your body

(A) THE PHYSICAL ENVIRONMENT

1. Declutter every six months.
2. Maintain a tidy, clean environment; throwing out and recycling to refresh your space.
3. Regularly open your windows and allow the flow of air through your property.
4. Bring life into your house with plants and fresh flowers; this creates the flow of oxygen.
5. Ensure you have no dead flowers or dead plants; dead-head and refresh water regularly.

(B) THE PHYSICAL BODY

1. Any form of stretching and gentle exercise; walking, yoga, t'ai chi.
2. Periods of fasting. Regular 12-hour fasting of no food between 7pm and 7am.
3. Not eating between meals and leaving 4 hours between meal times.
4. Alcohol and other toxic substances which overload the liver to be taken in moderation.
5. Drinking plenty of water.
6. Daily skin brushing – this improves the flow in the lymphatic system.

2. Psychological

The latest neurological research indicates that every human being has approximately 60,000 thoughts each waking day. It has further been suggested that 75 per cent of all thoughts are negative. We like to think that we choose our thoughts but the evidence suggests otherwise. There is a part of the brain where thoughts arise and a different part of the brain where we take immediate ownership of a thought as if we had selected it. The truth is that thoughts arise throughout the day in an uncontrolled manner, triggering two responses that create significant difficulty. The first is denial. In every family system and in every culture, certain areas of thought will be denied. In a religious family or system, for example, thoughts about sexuality might be denied, whereas in pacifist communities, aggressive or destructive thoughts might be denied. Equally, in families or communities where there is great attachment to being positive, any thoughts considered negative will be denied instantly.

At the other end of the spectrum, we are all familiar with the experience of latching on to specific thoughts and obsessing about them for hours or days to our detriment. We have created cultures that are highly addictive. The biggest addiction on our planet is the addiction to compulsive thinking. It is routine for all of us to obsess with thought in this way.

In either case, denial or attachment, there is no flow to the thoughts that are arising. The optimum way of being is to allow all thoughts, irrespective of their content, to flow through our mind and for us to observe the thought from a place of interest or curiosity. This idea has been at the heart of several spiritual traditions for thousands of years. It is not easy to adopt but a commitment to practise the art of allowing thoughts to flow is immensely beneficial.

Over the past decade, the practice of mindfulness has become extremely fashionable. Mindfulness embodies bringing our awareness to an experience, from a place of curiosity, without attachment. This practice can be immensely effective. However, many seeking to practise mindfulness fall into the trap of trying to be good at it. This creates yet one more egoistic activity. In the same way, a practitioner of yoga can become obsessed

It is important to
exist within an
environment that
encourages the
flow of ideas.

with doing the perfect headstand and downward dog, thus missing the point of yoga altogether.

In the arena of the psychological self, it is important to exist within an environment that encourages the flow of ideas. In some families, rigidity exists due to a dominating patriarch or matriarch, where it is 'my way or the highway'. Others in the family quickly learn that it is not safe to express original ideas. It is exactly the same in a work environment where a dogmatic and rigid boss seriously limits the creative potential of the employees and hence the company.

Our seed of intention will flourish and thrive within a flow of thought and openness to new and fresh ideas. Denying thoughts or ideas is akin to the neglect of our planted seed while attachment to thoughts or ideas, particularly around a specific outcome, is akin to agitation (overwatering) of our seed of intention. Both significantly limit and undermine the natural evolution of our intention.

3. Emotional

Most of us accept that we do not choose or control our emotions, in contrast to our thoughts, particularly intense emotions, such as anger or sadness. They can surge up unexpectedly and overwhelm us. Emotion arises from the gut and travels up through the chest. Our attitude to emotion varies considerably from culture to culture. For example, in the British culture we are notoriously unwelcoming of strong emotion, so our culturally inherited response is to deny it. The system of denial around emotion is much stronger in some families than in others.

Equally, certain emotions might be encouraged while others are not allowed. Sadness and fear, for example, might be acceptable in a family system whereas anger is completely unacceptable. Although significant progress has been made, there are still substantial gender differences around the tolerance of emotion.

Just as with thoughts, two different responses create and store up problems for the future. The habitual denial of emotion represses authentic impulses that are seeking expression. These are stored in the body and will lead to spontaneous uncontrollable outbursts or, worse still, physical illness. The other polarity is to attach to a particular feeling – for example, anger – and to become recognized as someone who is angry all the time. All of us have from time to time experienced the feeling of resentment, which literally means to 're-feel'. The word originates from the French *ressentir* – *re*, intensive prefix, and *sentir*, to feel – and from the Latin *sentire* (to feel). We churn the same emotion over and over and over again, which becomes deleterious to our emotional health.

Every thought and feeling affects our biochemistry. If we either deny or attach to that thought or feeling, we are storing up problems (blocks to our natural flow). It is not easy after decades of conditioning to allow emotions to flow in a natural and spontaneous way. It takes great commitment and practice to move forward and change a long-established habit. But if an intense emotion, such as anger, sadness or fear, is allowed to flow through the body, it is always surprising how quickly it rises and falls away, like a wave in

Every thought
and feeling affects
our biochemistry.

the ocean, and once it has dispersed, it is impossible to get it back. I regularly experience this. Unfortunately, this emotional flow has become counter-cultural for most of us, despite it being innately natural and healthy. However, it is possible to counteract harmful conditioning that blocks emotional flow. One way is to allow yourself to drop into the epicentre of the particular emotion arising. I find it helpful to imagine that I am willing to drown in the emotion, whether it is sadness, anxiety or anger. Inevitably, our thinking goes into overdrive and it is critical to bypass unhelpful thoughts and to focus awareness on the physical sensation in the body. This will encourage the emotion to flow.

Whenever a strong emotion arises, deep within us, there is a fear that the emotion will overwhelm us and maybe even destroy us. It feels like standing on the shore, becoming aware that a tsunami is approaching. Our instinct is to run away from it. This instinct is supported by layers of conditioning. If we could say to ourselves, 'I am going to stand firm and welcome the emotion, to allow the possibility of dying to the emotion' in reality it will pass through quickly. We will return to a feeling of peace and joy far sooner than we could ever imagine.

~

Trauma is a major inhibitor of flow. All human beings have suffered trauma and each of us is holding some unresolved trauma in our body that blocks our natural flow. All traumatic events are extremely stressful but all stressful events are not traumatic. Peter Levine, who is a world leader in trauma research, says, 'Trauma is the most avoided, ignored, denied, misunderstood, untreated cause of human suffering.' My own clinical practice supports this view. Firstly, trauma does not necessarily arise from a catastrophic event, as many people think; neither does it necessarily arise from a single event. Of course, war, childhood abuse, betrayal, abandonment, rape and serious illness can all cause traumas, but so too can minor car accidents, minor medical procedures, birth stress, natural disasters and sudden loud noises. A parent shouting at a child over a period of time can create trauma.

We become traumatized when our ability to respond to a *perceived* threat is overwhelming. Individuals can be traumatized by any event they *perceive* consciously or unconsciously to be life threatening. Trauma is about the loss of connection to ourselves, to our bodies, to our families, to others and to the world around us; hence it involves the absence of flow.

There are always two critical factors in the formation of trauma: the perception of threat and the incapacity to deal with it. When a situation is perceived to be life threatening, both mind and body mobilize a vast amount of energy in preparation for fight or flight. It is the same with all species. Once the perceived threat has passed, the discharge of energy from the body informs the brain that it is time to reduce the levels of stress hormones – the threat is no longer present. If this message to normalize is not given, the brain continues to release high levels of adrenalin and cortisol, so that the body holds on to its high-energy, ramped-up state.

Neurological research reveals that the instinctive parts of both human and animal brains are virtually identical. Only the rational part of our brain is uniquely human. If you observe any animal that has experienced a perceived threat, after the threat passes, the animal shakes out all the stored high-intensity energy and returns to calm. However, human beings are often scared of the intensity of their own energy and latent aggression – we brace ourselves against the power of the sensations, unwilling to discharge the pent-up energy. Undischarged energy is stored in the nervous system, creating a block and setting the stage for the formation of the symptoms of trauma.

In treating trauma, it is critical to understand that the condition is primarily physical, caused by something that occurred initially to our bodies and our instincts. The effects spread to our mind, emotions and spirit as a secondary process. Hence, in my experience, it is impossible to heal trauma through talking therapy. Many therapies re-traumatize by re-visiting the trauma rather than simply discharging the pent-up energy that is creating havoc with the adrenalin and corti- sol in the body. When we discharge the unresolved trauma through the expression of this stored-up energy, the body shakes, sometimes violently, and then we feel less threatened and overwhelmed by life. We feel more peaceful, at home with others, the world and ourselves. We are no longer trapped by events in our past, some of which we may not even remember.

There is one further aspect of trauma to consider. Any animal that is trapped in a situation where neither fight nor flight are viable options will freeze. Several species literally play dead as a way to avoid predators. Another vital function of the human organism that we share with other species is the ability to create numbness. If an impala or a human is killed while frozen, it will not suffer pain or even terror during its demise. If a human being experiences rape or some other violent and invasive attack, by freezing or becoming numb they limit the pain of the trauma at the time. Many human beings are walking around frozen or numb as a result of some unresolved trauma. There is no connection or flow within the body or

Connection to
the body gives
us a sense of
being alive and
of purpose in all
aspects of life.

with others. The mechanisms of our highly sophisticated organism, which protected us from intense pain, are no longer serving us.

The same solution as before is required to become unfrozen and to feel alive. We need to discharge the frozen and built-up repressed energy. Connection to the body gives us a sense of being alive and of purpose in all aspects of life. When we are disconnected from the body, we cannot be fully present. A meaningful life depends upon a sense of being alive and of presence, both of which spring from intimate contact with internal body states. Remember that the seed of intention is an inner impulse that arises from the body.

Shaking exercise

Stand with your feet firmly on the ground and then bounce up and down from your hips, bending your knees. Once you have established a rhythm, bring your arms in and shake them or punch the air with them.

When you are ready, you can bring your voice in to play and allow it to express itself in any way that you chose.

The second phase is to stomp around the house or preferably, bare foot in the garden on the grass, letting all your energy discharge downwards into the earth through the soles of your feet.

Five to ten minutes of this practice will radically transform stuck energy to lift your mood and vibration.

---

4. Spiritual

It is easy to observe that many spiritual and religious traditions are driven by great rigidity and dogma. All fundamentalism, whether it is Christian, Islamic, Judaic, Hindu or Buddhist, is contrary to flow. A strict reliance on religious text as opposed to open-ness to different layers of meaning is unhelpful to a sense of natural flow. The same applies to religious practice. If there is an unyielding punishing element to this, it is unlikely to be helpful to the overall well-being of the individual.

This equally applies to wellbeing practices, such as yoga, Pilates and meditation. For example, if I am going to yoga three or four times a week determined to do the perfect headstand or the optimum inversion, I am missing the point of yoga completely and am engaged in yet one more egoistic practice. In my clinical practice I have seen individuals who meditate for up to four hours a day. I often suggest their homework is to cease meditating for three weeks. There are only ever two reactions to this – either they become extremely angry and aggressive towards me or they find that they simply cannot or will not allow themselves to explore this. It is the same with a wide variety of practices.

Discipline and commitment are essential and to be highly valued, but when they spill over into rigidity and complete inflexibility, they cease to support overall wellbeing and become yet another block to flow.

Many people neglect their spiritual wellbeing. Some people might be hung up on the word spiritual, in which case we can substitute this with the word essence. Each one of us has an essence that is more than the sum of our parts. Equally, there is an existential way of being in the world. We need a sense of purpose, meaning and vision in our lives. Without this, we lack direction and evolution, so cease to support the essence of who we are. In my experience, people who have left behind the religious traditions of their youth and ancestors have an inner longing to discover a new path in life. It is important that we do not neglect this still quiet voice inside. Life is frenetic and intense. We need to allocate time to pause, and step out of the relentless pace of life in order to connect with our centre. Again, we need to avoid the two extremes of neglect and attachment. The optimum support for our seed of intention is beautifully encapsulated by the Buddhist invitation to 'wear life like a loose garment'.

5. Financial

When considering the importance of flow, it is impossible to ignore the role of money. One element of the seed of intention for the majority of people will relate, either directly or indirectly, to money and financial security. All of us have grown up in families and cultures with specific attitudes to money and wealth. Money is an energy in the same way that love or anger is an energy. We block the flow of money through a conscious or unconscious sense of lack (neglect) or over-attachment (hoarding.)

In 2008, the world came close to financial collapse. Several experts believe that we were far closer to complete financial meltdown than most people realize. A substantial coordinated response by the eight wealthiest governments on the planet averted disaster by pumping trillions of dollars into the system, a process that became known as quantitative easing. It is helpful to consider what actually caused the crisis. The global system of money is utterly dependent upon interbank lending. All the major banks in the world lend vast sums of money to each other on a daily basis. This is a requirement of the system.

In 2008, a growing awareness of strain and likely collapse created a fearful climate of damaging rumour. In a relatively short period of time, banks stopped lending to each other for fear of not being able to recover the debt. The system froze. If a global collapse had occurred, it would have arisen due to the lack of flow in the system. In 1900 it was calculated that 93 per cent of all money in issue was in circulation whereas a hundred years later, 92 per cent of all money in issue was not in circulation. If true, this means that only 8 per cent of the world's money circulates. Such a lack of flow creates significant risk for the system. It is exactly the same for our own individual financial position. If we are over-attached to money and hoard it, that actually inhibits the flow of money towards us. I am not, of course, advocating irresponsible over-spending. Once again, it is all a question of balance.

We need to achieve a healthy flow of money in and out of our accounts. In my experience, it is particularly difficult for people to understand and practise optimum balance in relation to money. A lot of old conditioning gets in the way. In my own life, there was a period recently when money was tight and my wife, who comes from a long background of financial lack, was both keen and anxious to curtail our spending. I, on the other hand, was determined to continue to spend in the confidence and trust that money would continue to flow. This is a subtle distinction and can easily be misunderstood and misused. My wife trusted my approach, despite her serious reservations, and over a period of two to three months, money began to flow more readily again.

Each situation is unique; prudent caution is appropriate but flow involves moving forwards with curiosity and confidence while staying open to what is possible. Whatever financial element is in your intention, it is important to apply the energy of flow and to be aware and attuned to the potential blocks.

Creating an Attractor Field

We exist in a culture where there is constant pressure to promote ourselves. We are encouraged to use more and more effort to arrive at where we are seeking to be. If instead of more promotion and more effort, we create an 'attractor field' aligned with our intention, then the desired outcome will arrive at our door in a much more efficient and effective way.

How to create an attractor field

1. Clarity of intention – the quality of the seed

2. Embody the intention (alignment) – watering and sunlight

3. Integrate the shadow – proficient weeding

4. Build confidence and trust – developing flow

Flow Meditation

(See page 185 for links to audio versions of the meditations.)

When you're ready, close your eyes and begin the process of withdrawing your attention from the outside and creating more awareness on the inside.

Begin by bringing awareness to the in-breath, the way in which the breath is effortlessly drawn into the body, and bringing a little more awareness to each and every in-breath – the way in which that breath enters your body.

And when you're ready, bring an equal amount of awareness to the out-breath, the way that you then return that breath to the atmosphere.

The breath flows in and the breath flows out. The tide comes in and the tide flows out in a never-ending cycle of flow.

And in your own time, I invite you to bring your

awareness to your heart, the physical heart. Now bring awareness to the beat of your heart and know that with every beat of your heart blood is sent around the 60,000 miles of blood vessels in your body. Blood is pumped out to all the capillaries, taking vital life energy all around your body. And exactly the same amount of blood that is sent out returns to the heart. There's a natural flow of blood from your heart whether you're awake or asleep, without your permission, without your control, blood is right now flowing through you.

Bring awareness to the natural, innate flow of your cardiovascular system, your circulatory system. If there is a small block in this system, high blood pressure results. If there is a major block, a heart attack results. Day and night there is an effortless flow without your awareness, without your permission and without your control.

And when you are ready, shift your awareness away from your heart to your digestive system; the miles and miles of the large intestine and the small intestine. Quietly, effortlessly, in this moment your digestive system is continuing to digest the last meal that you had, breaking down the food to supply vital nutrients, vitamins and minerals, to provide life to the cells in your body. Take a moment to honour this amazing system of digestion. Without your permission, without your control, there is a natural flow. Over the past ten to twenty years there's been a spate of digestive problems, such as irritable bowel syndrome. Each one of us is finding it difficult at times to digest life in its frenetic busyness.

Take a moment just to relax into, to admire with confidence, the beautifully simple, sophisticated system of digestion; the flow of food through your body. And now let go of that awareness, like watching a cloud pass through the sky.

Bring awareness to your endocrine system, the system in the body for communication via your hormones. Bring awareness to how complex this hormone balancing is, how well the natural flow of hormones throughout your body is regulated on a daily, hourly, minute-by-minute basis. Bring awareness to that process, that process of flow going on right now in this moment.

And when you are ready, in your own time, shift your

awareness to the respiratory system – the way that you draw breath into your lungs, the way that right now you are oxygenating your blood, bringing vital life energy into your body.

And on the out-breath you are letting go of carbon dioxide, on the in-breath breathing in vital oxygen, nourishing the white blood cells of your body, and on the out-breath effortlessly returning carbon dioxide to the atmosphere. Whether you are awake or asleep, the respiratory system is functioning, flowing through your body, maintaining health without your permission, without your control.

Once again, let go of your awareness like a cloud moving through the sky and shift this awareness to your autonomic nervous system. This system of flow collects and processes information from the senses via the nerves and the brain and informs our muscles to contract or to create a physical action. Even sitting, resting, our nervous system is regulating our whole body naturally, effortlessly. Information is flowing from the tip of our nose, to our chin, down through our torso, to our fingertips, down our legs, all the way to the tip of our big toes.

Bring awareness to that natural system of flow.

Now, in your own time, shift your attention to the flow of the lymphatic system. The process of drainage, whereby our body naturally rids us of toxins and waste.

There are hundreds of lymph nodes in the body. Bring your awareness to the spleen, the largest lymphatic organ, located on the left side of the body just above the kidney.

The spleen controls the amount of red blood cells and blood storage in the body to help us fight infection. Bring awareness to the flow through all the lymphatic nodes, which are consistently, regularly cleansing our body, healing our body of unwanted toxins, without our permission, without our control. There's no effort required, the flow is going on right now.

And now let your awareness of the lymphatic system fall away and bring your awareness to the immune system – the system in your body that fights disease. Constantly, your immune system is flowing through the body, fighting agents of disease, pathogens, viruses, parasitic worms, clearing the body of any agents of attack that are trying to destabilize the natural, innate, healthy organism that you are.

Take a moment to imagine a great shield around your body, an invisible shield that protects you from all outside advances. Imagine a few attacks bouncing off this shield, unable to get through. And now imagine the full artillery firing at you, the shells bouncing off this shield, unable to reach you because you're surrounded by the protective shield.

And now allow this shield to fall inwards, to collapse inwards inside your body and bring awareness to that flowing, moving shield of protection. Your immune system flows diligently, loyally, consistently, without your permission, without your effort, without your control, through your body, maintaining health.

Take a moment to bring awareness to all the systems of your body; the human organism is made up of many, many systems, all of which are in flow. All sickness, all disease is, in an important sense, an interruption to the natural, innate flow of the human organism. The human organism is probably the most sophisticated, self-healing organism that's ever existed. With a little support, the right nutrition, the appropriate exercise, this amazing organism – through flow – maintains a level of vitality, a level of vibrancy and wellbeing. Without constant effort, without relentless busyness.

Just in this moment fall into a place of trust and confidence in the natural flow of your body.

And just as the Universe around you is made up of the same natural, healthy, flowing systems, the water, the rain, the sunlight will nourish, will nurture, the seed of your intention, helping your intention to flower into its true magnificence, to reach its potential through a simple system of allowing flow.

In your own time, very slowly open your eyes and bring your attention back into the room where you are sitting.

SIX

HARVEST

I t is time to reap the harvest. We have planted our seed of intention, we have provided sufficient sunlight and water and we have undertaken diligent weeding. We have also learned about the importance of flow in nature and ourselves. Scientists tell us that the universe is expanding. In this expanding universe there is infinite possibility. However, each one of us lives our life each day with a litany of limiting beliefs and limiting possibilities. The power of intention is that it enables us to enter into the realm of what is possible.

Probably the most damaging limiting belief is to make other people responsible for our lives. We do this in myriad ways. We have created a culture where most of us are addicted to complaining on a daily basis. Each time we complain about something or someone, we are giving that person or thing responsibility for our lives.

Our lives are made up of millions of events. Some are mundane and ordinary – we get up in the morning, drink a cup of tea, have a shower and get dressed. Other events are more significant – we buy houses, get married, have children and get divorced. Then there are even more seismic events, such as the death of our loved ones, serious injuries and catastrophic accidents. After decades of reflection, it seems to me that with all of these events, there are only ever two possibilities for a response. Either we see life as happening *to* us or we see life as happening *for* us. The dominant cultural zeitgeist is for most of us to see life as happening to us. Road accidents happen, people break into our houses and we lose our jobs. We even have expressions that reflect this dominant view, such as 'she was dealt a difficult set of cards', or 'he was unlucky in love'. The difficulty with this approach is that it means we are like a cork bobbing in the ocean at the whim and mercy of life. Long ago I concluded that if this was the case, it was not a life worth living.

———

The alternative is to discover that life happens for us insofar as each event is an opportunity to evolve. Obviously, events that are desirable and pleasurable are accepted as welcome, whereas events that are undesirable, difficult and painful are hard to welcome. Frequently, we gain the greatest growth from the latter.

To develop the idea of life happening for us a step further, it is possible to see that we create (or at the very least co-create) the life we are living. We have looked at this through the lens of the filter and through the projector, where science clearly demonstrates that each one of us creates our reality all the time. It is also easy to understand that if we are feeling angry and bitter as we go through the day, we tend to attract conflict and aggression. Equally, if we are light-hearted and happy, we tend to attract more positive situations towards ourselves.

The critical step in moving from limited thinking to infinite thinking is understanding and accepting that we are responsible for the reality we create. Without this, we are more likely to stay stuck. If we realize that we create a particular reality through finite thinking, it becomes possible to create a different reality through different thinking. We can then imagine what might become possible using infinite thinking.

~

All human beings limit their potential with a series of largely unrecognized finite beliefs. A limiting belief is something that constrains us in some way. We have limiting beliefs about our identity, other people, organizations, cultures, gender and the make-up of the world. The two simplest and most damaging examples of limiting beliefs are 'I can't' and 'I don't know how'. I often ask individuals to undertake homework by allocating one particular day to listen to how many times they hear themselves and others use the word 'can't'.

The critical step
in moving from
limited thinking to
infinite thinking is
understanding and
accepting that we
are responsible for
the reality we create.

> There are not too many guarantees in life but every time we say 'I can't', we are guaranteed to stay where we are.

It is surprising and shocking to discover how over-used this expression is. In more than 90 per cent of cases when we say 'I can't', it is really a substitute for the truth, which is 'I won't' or 'I don't want to'. The list of things that we cannot do as individuals is much shorter than we would like to think. We spend our lives constantly limiting what is possible in many different ways without really taking stock of what we are doing. It is as if we are in a hypnotic state while at the same time giving the responsibility to someone or something else.

Henry Ford, who built motorcars, was neither a psychologist nor a philosopher but he once said, 'Whether you think you can or you can't, you are right.' This expression is widely applicable to life. If we believe that we cannot drive a car, learn a foreign language, have a happy marriage, earn more money, then we most certainly won't. If we believe that we can climb a tree, write a book, play a musical instrument or be a great parent, we almost certainly will.

The second most limiting belief, in my experience – 'I don't know how' – is similar to 'I can't' in being guaranteed to keep us stuck. I regularly encounter people saying, 'I want to change this or I want to change that but I don't know how.' This is a deception and a delusion. The truth is that they do not want to make the change because the familiar is too comfortable. This is because human beings and in particular the human brain operate as a 'pattern recognition programme', i.e. with every new situation or scenario encountered, two questions always arise: 1. 'Have I seen this before?' and 2. 'Is this safe or a threat?' The familiar is to be safe, i.e. we survived and hence highly prized. This is why people sit in the same place and gravitate towards what is familiar. To say 'I don't know how' has become a convenient cop-out. If we don't know how, we can always find out. The world is full of experts and information has never been easier to access, although the deeper truth is that we do not need to know how in order to realize or manifest something. It is sufficient to know that it is possible. Consider again the acorn and the pumpkin seed. They do not know cognitively how to become an oak tree or a pumpkin but they do contain everything necessary to ensure that this will happen.

The list of limiting beliefs is endless and includes 'I do', 'I don't', 'I am' and 'I am not'. We often define ourselves by what we do or do not do. For example, if I define my identity as being a logical, rational person, I will convince myself that I am not creative or artistic. Equally, if I create an identity around being creative and artistic, I may well exclude the possibility of being organized and self-disciplined. Every time we accept a particular characteristic, such as being measured and cautious, we exclude other possibilities, such as being impulsive and a risk taker. The truth is that we can have all possibilities available to us for different scenarios.

Every time I am teaching or working with a group of people, there are always one or two individuals who say that they love change. I never believe them.

Having worked with clients for over 30 years, I am more convinced than ever that human beings do not like or welcome change. We seek the familiar and maintain homeostasis at all costs. The greatest catalyst for change is crisis. Any crisis creates an opening and willingness to see things differently and offers the opportunity to move forward. Change is an iterative process, which takes place over a period of time. I suggest that the 'how' of change is honesty, openness and willingness. All change begins with a greater degree of honesty, usually self-honesty, than is the norm.

> We need to be more honest about our delusions, distortions and denials. Greater honesty is the same as awareness. Without this, it is difficult to move forward.

In common with honesty, openness is critical. All change requires us to move beyond what we think we know. We have grown up with the mantra that

Once we have cultivated more honesty and openess, we need to be willing to choose differently.

knowledge is power and in certain arenas, this might well be the case. However, all knowledge eventually becomes a prison that keeps us trapped. Openness requires us to suspend what we think we know and be open to other possibilities. We are quick to highlight dogmas in others but not so ready to acknowledge dogmas within ourselves.

Once we have cultivated more honesty and openness, we need to be willing to choose differently. Without a willingness to overcome ingrained habits and past patterns that have become limiting or, worse still, destructive, we will continue to choke our potential.

Another area that substantially limits our potential is the litany of shoulds and shouldn'ts based on values, cultural norms, laws and other rules that constrain what we should or shouldn't do. We may well choose to retain some of these shoulds and shouldn'ts but in every case it is helpful and beneficial to change 'I should' to 'I choose to' and 'I shouldn't' to 'I choose not to'. In this way, it becomes expansive rather than limiting. For example, we might carry a belief that we shouldn't be competitive. The more we hear the 'shouldn't' in our internal dialogue, the more it creates a prohibition and an enforced barrier through which we cannot move. Whereas if, after reflection, we decide that we choose not to be competitive, it is an active decision, which is expansive because it brings greater internal or external reward. In choosing not to be competitive, we find ourselves being more collaborative and working alongside others, which is satisfying and rewarding.

In addition to the previous limiting beliefs, which are about ourselves, we all have many limiting beliefs about other people and the world in general. For example, we might think that other people cannot be trusted. Similarly, we might have conscious or unconscious limiting beliefs about gender – men are unreliable and women are emotional. Other common limiting beliefs that we all share are 'bad things happen', 'life is out to get you', 'success never lasts', 'life is unfair'.

⸻

When I reflect on what the dominant energy operating on the planet might be, I always get a strong sense that it is lack. We run our lives on the explicit or implicit assumption that there is not enough. There is not enough money, not enough land, not enough food, not enough fresh water, not enough love, not enough joy, not enough forgiveness – the list is endless. We have created cultures that are always looking for more and are essentially addictive. If you look at North America or Western Europe as an individual, it is easy to see how the collective has become an addict who can never get enough, relentlessly seeking the next fix. Most of the structures that we have created are based on this assumption of lack. For example, capitalism is dependent upon competition being seen as necessary and highly desirable because there is not enough for everyone. There are, however, a small minority of individuals who wake every morning with the inner knowledge that there is enough of everything – enough money, enough food, enough hours in the day, enough love. Pause for a second and imagine what your life might look like if each day you had this innate confidence that there was enough, an abundant harvest.

~

Another key factor that determines the quality and quantity of the harvest, related to finite thinking, is the level of disconnection within ourselves and each other. We have created cultures that bring about an epidemic of disconnection. The ways in which we disconnect from ourselves include taking prescribed medication, excessive use of alcohol, recreational drugs, pornography, over-eating, busyness and overwork. It is less commonly understood that any spiritual practice, for example, yoga, meditation or chanting, can create greater disconnection due to becoming yet one more egoistic practice rather than encouraging more connection and expansion.

During my lifetime we have created the internet, which now appears to connect several billion people. Yet my sense is that overall it has brought about far greater disconnection. None of us need reminding of

Imagine what
your life might
look like if each
day you had this
innate confidence
that there was
enough.

the compulsive overuse of mobile phones and other digital devices.

50 per cent of young people admit to mobile phone addiction, 68 per cent of adults sleep with their phones near the bed, 40 per cent of users check their mobile phones in the toilet, 12 per cent of adults use their phones in the shower, 20 per cent of 18–34 year olds used their mobile phones during sex, 50 per cent of users feel uneasy when they leave phones at home, 26 per cent of all car accidents are caused by phone usage and 56 per cent of parents check their devices while driving.

All of my work, whether with individuals or with organizations large and small, draws upon science and spirituality in equal measure. Both these arenas have one fundamental thing in common. Since the very beginning, science, and more particularly physics, has been focused on discovering the ultimate nature of reality. Spirituality, and in particular mysticism, is also primarily interested in the ultimate reality of what exists. Physics dissected life, quite literally, in its pursuit of the ultimate building blocks of reality. We arrived at the atom, which was at the time considered by scientists to be the answer. The atom was then split to reveal a world of subatomic particles – neutrons, electrons, protons. We then developed quantum mechanics, waves and particles; quantum mechanics developed into quantum field theory and we are currently confronted with a number of competing superstring theories.

The clear suggestion is emerging from the scientific world that the fundamental truth about the universe is everything is connected. Scientists refer to the El Niño effect – a climate cycle in the Pacific Ocean that has a global impact on weather patterns. The suggestion is that a butterfly in one part of the world flaps its wings and eventually the consequences are felt on the other side of the planet. From a completely different starting point and wide-ranging religious backgrounds, including

One way to
ensure an
abundant harvest
is to create
greater
connection
with ourselves
and others.

Judaism, Christianity, Hinduism and Buddhism, every mystic reports the same underlying reality that everything is one, based on interconnectivity. Indigenous people of different traditions, such as Native Americans, Aboriginals and Hopi Indians, have maintained this simple truth for thousands of years.

One way to ensure an abundant harvest is to create greater connection with ourselves and others. The more connected we are, the more aligned we will be with the cosmos. This alignment will guarantee abundance. We noted that the route to healing from all trauma is to re-establish this innate, natural sense of connection with our self, others and the world around us. Our seed of intention was discovered by reflecting more deeply within ourselves, by being more connected with our bodily sensations, our dreams and longing. Once we discover this and articulate it clearly and powerfully, we set about embodying it in every cell in our body – we create even greater connection to this natural, innate impulse. We then diligently, with commitment and discipline, address what gets in the way.

Here is a simple roadmap to help you reconnect:

The body never lies. It is a direct line of communication to your instincts and will always tell you honestly what is best for you and what needs shifting. You need to choose to listen.

Scan the body; what are the sensations you notice?

For example, tightness, pulling, dark, hollow, expanding, fluttery, dense, blocked, tense, closed, open, clenched, sweaty, calm…

As you notice the sensations in your body, also wonder, what is your body telling you?

Allow any feelings to rise and pass through like a cloud in the sky. What are these feelings telling you?

Take a moment to breathe into each of your centres – your gut, your heart and your head. What do you notice?

When you follow your inner knowing, and act on the information your body is giving you, you will step into another level of being that will carry more integrity and power.

If we plant a pumpkin seed, we get a pumpkin. If we plant a sunflower seed, with a modest amount of sunlight, water and weeding, we get a sunflower. It is essential to understand that if we have conscientiously discovered our intention and aligned this with the cosmos, through the commitment and discipline of removing the obstacles that get in the way (weeding), the outcome is predetermined and guaranteed. The only person or thing that can stop our intention from becoming reality is ourself. If we understand this simple truth, we are indeed masters of our own destiny and capable of creating the life we choose. It is not the quick fix that our culture has conditioned us to expect. It is a lifelong practice of developing awareness, commitment and discipline. Any gardener knows that considerable time and energy goes into preparing the soil, planting in the right season, ensuring sufficient sunlight and water are available – all of which, along with constant weeding, produce a bountiful harvest.

Chapter Two

Mind mapping: Tony Buzan: https://imindmap.com/ or Rico Clusters https://www.lifehack.org/articles/featured/rico-clusters-an-alternative-to-mind-mapping.html

The audio recordings of all the meditations can be found on Andrew's website: www.themoderndaywizard.org

Chapter Five

Find out more about Marie Kondo at: https://konmari.com/. Peter Levine's work, known as 'Somatic Experiencing' is carried out through the Foundation for Human Enrichment. More information and resources can be found at www.traumahealing.com

Chapter Six

https://www.dailyinfographic.com/15-terrifying-statistics-about-cell-phone-addiction

BIBLIOGRAPHY

Allport, Gordon, *Pattern and Growth in Personality* (Harcourt College Publishing, 1961)

Bohm, David, *The Undivided Universe* (Routledge, 1995)

Bohm, David, *Wholeness and the Implicate Order* (Routledge, 2002)

Bohm, David, *The Essential David Bohm* (Routledge, 2003)

Chisolm, Hugh (ed.), 'Rubicon' *Encyclopedia Britannica* (11th ed.) (Cambridge University Press, 1922)

Chopra, Dr Deepak, *Quantum Healing* (New York: Bantam Books, 1989)

Chopra, Dr Deepak, *The Seven Spiritual Laws of Success* (Amber Allen Publishing and New World Library, 1994)

Chopra, Dr Deepak, *Synchrodestiny: Harnessing the Infinite Power of Coincidence to Create Miracles* (Rider, 2005)

Chopra, Dr Deepak, *The Soul of Leadership* (New York: Harmony Books, 2008)

Cook, Blanche Wiesen, *Eleanor Roosevelt, Vol. 2: 1933–1938* (Viking, 1999)

Dolan, Paul, *Happiness by Design: Change What You Do, Not How You Think* (New York: Hudson Street Press, 2014)

Dolan, Paul, *Happiness by Design: Finding Pleasure and Purpose in Everyday Life* (Penguin, 2015)

Drake, Stillman, *The Discoveries and Opinions of Galileo* (First Anchor Books, 1957)

D'Souza, Steven and Renner, Diana, *Not Knowing: The Art of Turning Uncertainty into Possibility* (LID Publishing, 2014)

Ellwood, Robert and Alles, Gregory, *The Encyclopedia of World Religions* (Facts on File)

Fendall, Arthur, *All Things Natural: Ficino on Plato's Timaeus* (Shepheard-Walwyn (Publishers) Ltd, 2010)

Fogelin, Robert J, *The Cambridge Companion to Quine* (Cambridge University Press, 2004)

Forman, Lillian E, *Albert Einstein: Physicist and Genius* (Abdo Publishing Company, 2010)

Gorbachev, Mikhail Sergeyevich, *Memoirs* (Doubleday, 1996)

Jeal, Tim, *Explorers of the Nile* (Yale University Press, 2011)

Juul, Jesper, *Your Competent Child – Towards New Basic Values for the Family* (New York: Farrar, Straus and Giroux, 2001)

Kahneman, D, Diener, E, & Schwarz, N (eds), *Well-being: The Foundations of Hedonic Psychology* (New York: Russell Sage Foundation, 1999)

Kahneman, Daniel, *Thinking, Fast and Slow* (Penguin, 2012)

Kahneman, Daniel and Tversky, Amos, *Choices, Values and Frames* (Cambridge University Press, 2000)

Kalckar, Jorgen (ed.), *Volume 6 Foundations of Quantum Physics I (1926–1932) Niels Bohr Collected Works* (Amsterdam: Elsevier, 2008)

Kalckar, Jorgen (ed.), *Volume 7 Foundations of Quantum Physics I (1926–1932) Niels Bohr Collected Works* (Amsterdam: Elsevier, 2008)

Kuhn, Thomas S, *The Capernican Revolution* (Harvard University Press, 1957)

Pais, Abraham, *Subtle is the Lord: The Science and the Life of Albert Einstein* (Oxford University Press, 1982)

Pasternak, Charles, *Quest: The Essence of Humanity* (John Wiley & Sons, 2004)

Planck, Max, *A Survey of Physical Theory* (Dover Publications, 1993)

Planck, Max, *The Origin and Development of the Quantum Theory* (Forgotten Books, 2016)

Pribram, Karl H, *Brain and Perception: Holonomy and Structure in Figural Processing* (Psychology Press, 1991)

Pribram, Karl H, *The Form Within* (Prospecta Press, 2013)

Quine, Willard Van Orman, *Two Dogmas of Empiricism* (*The Philosophical Review* 60: 20–43, 1951)

Quine, Willard Van Orman, *Ontological Relativity and Other Essays* (Columbia University Press, 1977)

Russell, Jeffrey Burton, *Inventing the Flat Earth: Columbus and Modern Historians* (New York: Praeger, 1991)

Sober, Elliott, *Ockham's Razor: A User's Manual* (Cambridge University Press, 2015)

Talbot, Michael, *The Holographic Universe* (HarperCollins, 1996)

Talbot, Michael, *Part 1 Complete – Synchronicity and the Holographic Universe – Thinking Allowed* (uploaded on 18 December 2010 www.thinkingallowed.com)

Wilber, Ken, *The Spectrum of Consciousness* (Quest Books, 1993)

Wilber, Ken, *A Theory of Everything* (Gateway, 2001)

ACKNOWLEDGEMENTS

I would like to acknowledge my father, Brian Stanley, and my mother, Shirley Carol, without whose intention I would not be here and this book would not have been written. I would like to acknowledge and thank Carol, Nigel, Sally and Patrick for choosing to share this lifetime with me. Also, my thanks and appreciation to Katherine, Elizabeth, Victoria and Daisy for their intention to be my teachers in this life.

I would like to thank the many friends and colleagues whose intention to support and challenge me has enriched my life greatly.

Huge thanks and appreciation to Kate Adams at Aster and her entire team, Sophie Elletson for invaluable editing, Juliette Norsworthy for beautiful design work, Lisa Pinnell for production and Meg Brown and Caro Parodi for publicity and marketing – all of whom have contributed to making this a far better book than it might otherwise have been.

And finally, but by no means least, to my lovely wife, Anna, who is adorable and annoying in equal measure and whose intention to appear in my life has been the greatest challenge and the most brilliant experience imaginable. Without her, it is impossible that this book would have been written because with her by my side, I have absolutely no intention of developing more self-discipline in this lifetime.

ABOUT THE AUTHOR

Andrew Wallas has been described in the *Daily Mail* as a 'modern-day wizard' who 'transforms your energy'. He has been successful in an outer world sense but was ahead of the curve in realizing 32 years ago that real wealth is not money, it is happiness. Just as real value isn't about bank balances; it's about fulfilment, love, passion, freedom and joy.

His aim is to impart the message that if we concentrate on our inner world, our outer world will reflect any internal shift we make. His powerful and inspirational work embodies the notion that joy is readily available now. Where his essence and personality meet, he shows us through his own open-heartedness and implicit understanding of our universal struggles, how to lead a graceful and loving life. He's an inspirational character with a fearless individuality who underlines the folly of constructing a false self and shows us how to best be and accept our true authentic self.